GOURD CRAFT

GOURD CRAFT

Growing, Designing, and Decorating Ornamental and Hardshelled Gourds

by CAROLYN MORDECAI

Dedicated to my son and daughter
Diane and Lenny and my Aunt Dorothy.

© Carolyn Mordecai 1978

AMERICAN GOURD SOCIETY, INC.,
P. O. BOX 274
MT. GILEAD, OHIO 43338-0274
(419) 946-3302

Printed in the United States of America
Published by the AMERICAN GOURD SOCIETY, INC.

Designed by Rhea Braunstein

Library of Congress Cataloging in Publication Data

Mordecai, Carolyn
GOURD CRAFT

Bibliography:
Includes index
1. Gourd craft. 2. Gourds. I. Title
TT880.M65 First Edition   1978   745.5   77-25870
Second Edition 1989
ISBN 0-9623516-0-1

Printed by The Hartman Printing Co., Mt. Gilead, Ohio

Contents

Acknowledgments

Finding information on gourds in well-hidden nooks and crannies of libraries and museums is like playing hide-and-seek. Being "it" turned out to be a rewarding task after finding new friends who so generously contributed to this book.

First of all, I wish to pay tribute to three expert gourd artists to whom I am deeply indebted:

My good friend, Minnie Black—Kentucky gourd sculptor—who added much humor, spice, and talent to this crafts book.

Larue Stith, who shared his exquisite burning techniques for decorating gourds, as well as his final results.

Mathematics professor Dr. Leslie Miller, excellent gourd carver, whose mathematical ability is demonstrated in his designs that cover the gourd's surface.

Also, I am especially grateful to Marvin Johnson of Fuquay Varina, North Carolina, for an opportunity to photograph a variety of gourd crafts in his private museum. Mr. Johnson, also a gourd cultivator, provided me with many of the larger gourds that were crafted and illustrated in this book.

It would have been impossible to cover the African Nigerian methods of crafting without the help and contributions of anthropologist Dr. Barbara Rubin of Los Angeles.

My sincere thanks go to Robert Wiess of Raquel's Collection in Great Neck, New York, for permission to take pictures of beautiful Peruvian gourds. Thanks to Carol Long, manager of the Carnegie Museum Shop, for allowing the photography of the Peruvian Collection as well as African gourds.

In addition, I am grateful to the Mexican Folk Art Annex in New York City for selecting representative samples of Mexican gourd art and for permitting them to be photographed. Thanks to Anne O'Neill.

It was an unexpected pleasure to receive photographs of growing and crafted gourds from John Kraft of Sweden. Thanks to Mr. Kraft for his wonderful contributions.

A special thanks goes to Gary Feuerstein, talented artist, for taking his valuable time to illustrate with pen and ink the accomplishments of the Oregon Gourd Society.

My special thanks to Señorita de Saco of the Museo Nacional de la

ACKNOWLEDGEMENTS

Cultura Peruana for her kind cooperation and explanation of Peruvian gourd art during various periods of history. I am grateful to the National Museum of Peruvian Culture for permission to print photographs of Peruvian gourds. Thanks to Senor Wilfred Loaza for his labor on photographs of work accomplished by Peruvian artists.

The British Museum in London was exceptionally helpful via providing pictures and information concerning their collections. Thanks to G.S. Barker and the trustees of the museum. My thanks go to many others for their special contributions:

Gourd artists and craftspeople:

Eugene Deardorff	Jaimie and Craig Mock
Karen Feuerstein	Glenn Swenson
Thomas and Eileen Holt	E. P. Wallace
John Kraft	Mildred and Lowell Welch
Craig Lewis	Ralph Schneider
Marvin Johnson	Dr. Leslie Miller
(for supplying gourds)	Larue Stith
	Minnie Black

Photographic Contributions:

African Arts Magazine	O. C. Stevens
Sara Blixt	John Stevens
Sergio Carvajal	J. S. Story
Agnes Lorentzou	Eleanor Therien
Smithsonian Institution	

Translators:

Ted Goodman

Typist:

Helen Murphy

I am extremely gratified and happy that The Gourd Society of America, Inc. has published the second edition and subsequent printings of this book My thanks goes to Wilda M. Vogelhuber, American Gourd Society President, for enthusiastically coordinating the many steps to create this new publication.

Introduction

This book covers mainly Lagenaria, large Hardshelled gourds, which historically have been used throughout the world as containers. Of all gourds, the large Lagenaria are most suitable for crafting and decorating. These large gourds grow into a variety of shapes and sizes for almost every utilitarian purpose. Their green fruits dry to hard, thick, and woody shells. If given proper care, the cured gourd will last for years.

Many people are not aware that they can grow and decorate "containers" from their own backyards. Though tropical in origin, Lagenaria can be grown successfully in temperate regions. Instructions for the cultivation of Hardshelled gourds are given in chapter 3.

Though the bulk of the text focuses mainly on Lagenaria, one chapter primarily deals with Ornamental gourds. Small Ornamentals are the numerous types of brightly colored and patterned gourds widely used at harvesttime as seasonal decoration. Many dry to a natural, thin shell, less durable than the wall of the Lagenaria. Ornamentals have their place in the crafting of human, animal, and sculptural forms—and for adorning wreaths and plaques.

Raising Lagenarias and Ornamental gourds is similar to growing other familiar plants having long running vines: squash, cucumbers, melons, and pumpkins. All are members of the Cucurbitaceae family and are easy to cultivate. It is interesting and pleasurable to watch the gourds take shape as they mature. Their unpredictable form and characteristic beauty provide a challenge to the imagination.

After gourds are harvested and become dry, they can be fashioned into any number of decorative and useful objects: vases, canisters, bowls, contemporary sculpture, floral arrangements, human and animal sculptures, jewelry, lamps, and musical instruments. A general knowledge of crafting and decorating gourds is covered in chapters 4 and 5. These chapters suggest basic tools and many techniques of working with gourds. Subsequent chapters show projects being created using the methods in chapters 4 and 5. These illustrated techniques are interchangeable and can be used with many types of gourd projects.

The text also features traditional ways of crafting and applying designs from countries around the world. Should you wish to employ established techniques still flourishing throughout the globe, you may try

Mexican lacquering or beading, Peruvian carving and burning, or African pyro-engraving (burning) or pressure-engraving (carving).

Given equal coverage are contemporary and innovative techniques, worked out for modern craftspeople: gourd sculpturing, interpretive floral arranging, batiking, weaving, and appliquéing methods. Modern processes, such as carving with electrical power tools and burning with a propane torch, are included as well for ease of crafting.

Costly tools are not needed for crafting gourds. Openings in the gourd may be cut with a pocket or paring knife; ornamentation can be carved with a sharpened screw driver—similar to the African or Peruvian carving implements. Embellishment of gourds using simple tools is still prevalent in countries of Central and South America and in Africa, in areas where people still live close to the earth.

Once regarded as a minor art, the crafting and decorating of the calabash is now receiving major treatment. The book *In Praise of Hands* of the World Crafts Council devotes several pages to the decorating of Hardshelled gourds.

In modern technological societies the need still exists to receive pleasure and fulfillment from the fruits of nature. The growing and decorating of gourds is the latest exciting challenge for crafts lovers. Where else can a canister, planter, or bowl be obtained more inexpensively than one cultivated by man and nourished by nature?

GOURD CRAFT

A honey brown Lagenaria is decorated with a carved and painted Peruvian motif. Small areas and pathways of the design are painted with bright colors: red, blue, green, white, and black. Courtesy, Museum of Marvin Johnson

The Development of Contemporary Gourd Art

Gourds are the fascinating pottery of the plant world. There is a shape for almost every utilitarian purpose. When the fruit of the plant is functional, it is usually called a "calabash," "calabaza," or "mati" in Spanish-speaking countries. Though gourds have been used and decorated for centuries in various parts of the world, they have received little attention by anthropologists and historians who study the arts of mankind. Economic botanists, who are concerned with the kinds of plants useful to man, rarely include gourds in their literature.

The botanical history and distribution of gourds is still a mystery. The reasons are because of the great antiquity of the plant and its wide and unusual distribution. Ancient cultivation of gourds is reported in Africa, Mexico, South America, and Egypt. Evidence of the beginnings is so conflicting that it is safe to say that the origins of the plant are still unknown.

Some geological authorities believe that the bridge of Northwest Africa fits into the Western Hemisphere next to Mexico and other Central American countries. Eventually, the plates of Africa and the Western Hemisphere were spread apart as the ocean developed between the continents. Because gourds are historically prevalent in Northwest Africa and Central America, the conclusion is that the nature of the ever-changing movements of the earth helped distribute gourds to various parts of the world.

Another fascinating theory is that gourds were distributed from one continent to another "on the crest of a wave" by oceanic currents. Bottle gourds and other Lagenaria float easily because they are light in weight and have a durable, waterproof shell. In the 1960s Dr. Thomas Whitaker and Dr. George F. Carter reported that they floated Bottle gourds for 347 days, then stored the gourds for one year. After planting seeds from these gourds, 24 percent still germinated. Though gourds could have been distributed by oceanic currents, there is no proof that they did.

The final assumption is that people, seeing the obvious use of the Lagenaria Bottles, Kettles, Dippers, etc., distributed growth of new gourd plants as they migrated.

At any rate, the oldest Bottle gourd material in our Western Hemisphere is radiocarbon dated as far back as 12,000 B.C. Pieces of probably wild Lagenaria were excavated in Ayacucho, Peru. The oldest Bottle gourd associated with human use, found in the Ocampo Caves in the Mexican state of Tamalipas, is dated 7000 B.C.

Both Egypt on the African continent and Peru yielded evidence from the fourth millennium B.C. Specimens of gourd were found in the Egyptian tomb of the Fifth Dynasty. They were used as storage containers to help the deceased on his journey. Junius Bird found abundant material in Huaca Prieta on the northern coast of Peru. The strata dated about 2,500 B.C. Intact gourds attached to fishing nets indicated they were used by the Peruvian Indians as floats, as they still are today. Although many undecorated gourds were uncovered at this site, two carved gourds were present.

From the past to the present calabashes have served as useful vessels, utensils, and musical instruments in Asia, Africa, Central and South America, the islands of the South Pacific, and the Caribbean Islands. In these areas flasks, dippers, and other gourd containers were and still are being decorated by tribal artists.

Countries known to have used gourds for centuries or for certain periods in their history are Japan, China, Burma, Russia, India, Ceylon, New Zealand, and countries along the Mediterranean Sea. In Japan Bottle gourds were intricately carved or lacquered to be used as containers for sake (wine). Hawaiians used huge basket gourds for storing seed. Their mature gourds, often weighing a hundred pounds, were reduced to only a couple of pounds when dry.

The Chinese grew gourds in small clay molds. Their smooth perfected shapes were often finely decorated with a relief incised in the wall of a clay mold. The gourds, used to hold crickets for gambling purposes, are now almost extinct in that part of the world. Evidence of the Chinese Cricket gourds still can be seen at Salem's Peabody Museum and at the private museum of Mr. Johnson in Fuguay Varina, North Carolina.

In Russia and Burma calabashes were lavishly decorated with silver incised designs. In India musical instruments, various types of sitars, were played using gourds as resonators. Gourd rafts were used in India to cross the Ganges River. At present, gourd wine bottles are still being beautifully engraved in Ceylon.

At one time gourds played a utilitarian role in the daily life of the Polynesians. Since clay for making ceramics was absent from their volcanic soil, gourds provided the very necessary containers and utensils.

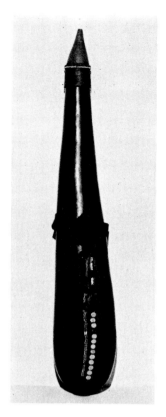

Gourd flask with handle and stopper. Courtesy, Museum of Marvin Johnson

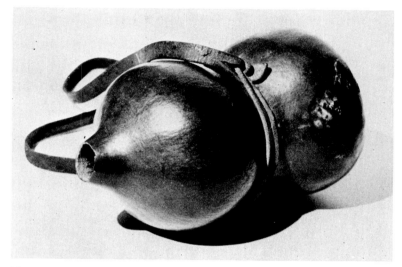

Mexican water jug. Bottle gourd water jugs with leather thong or rope handles have been used for centuries in Central and South American countries. Courtesy, Museum of Marvin Johnson

Gourd canteen with leather straps. Brad Jannelli. Illustrated by Gary Feuerstein

Chinese Cricket gourd. This shapely smooth-walled gourd was grown in a clay mold in ancient China. The intricately carved lid was made to rest on the ivory rim of the container. The Chinese Cricket gourd was used to hold crickets for gambling purposes. Courtesy, Museum of Marvin Johnson

Carved Maori gourd. The winding decorative motif represents the traditional designs of the Maori Indians of New Zealand. Theo Schoon. Courtesy, Museum of Marvin Johnson

The Maori tribe of New Zealand grew gourds—or "hue"—as containers for water, wild honey, and for meat (rats, pigeons, tuis, and human flesh) preserved in its own fat. Gourds were valued so much that they expended much time and effort to grow them well. Seeds were planted in a ritualistic manner after a full moon. The planter faced the east with a seed in each hand, raised his arms, and motioned the shape he wished the gourds to grow. Then he planted the seed.

Besides using them as containers, the Maori picked gourds while they were green and cooked them as vegetables. Other uses for gourds include musical instruments such as trumpets and flutes, lamps, floats, and fishing nets. The gourd became a humming top by inserting a stick through a small gourd and boring a few holes in its side. There were contests to see which gourd would hum the loudest. Of all the gourds used by the Maori, only the ones belonging to the chiefs were decorated. A few of these gourds are exhibited at the Dominion Museum in Wellington, New Zealand.

Though the traditional Maori gourds became almost extinct, Theo Schoon and Pine Taiapa emerged as gourd growers and carvers in the 1960s. Theo Schoon's designs are based on the long winding Maori designs of the past. Being in the Southern Hemisphere, these growers and carvers plant their gourds at the beginning of August, after the risk of frost has passed.

Sweden and Denmark are the newest countries to proudly add to the list of gourd-growing nations. The Lagenaria was introduced to the countries of northern Europe during the early 1970s and has been on trial for several years. Since the climate in Finland and northwestern Sweden is favorably influenced by central Asiatic high pressures, warm sunny weather generally prevails during the summers. It is hard to believe that tropical Lagenarias are fruiting as far north as Luleå, about 150 kilometers south of the polar circle, to Vasa, Finland. Pollination is done manually to ensure the earliest possible fruit setting. The Swedish calabash is decorated with electric soldering copper, India ink, paint, or a glowing needle.

Swedish calabashes are decorated with a soldering copper. Courtesy, John Kraft

Agnes Lorentzou of Sweden is holding a Lagenaria grown about 150 kilometers from the Arctic Circle. Courtesy, John Kraft

Many countries in Central and South America and in Asia and Africa have grown and decorated gourds for centuries. The following pages cover major countries actively engaging in gourd crafts: Nigeria, Ghana, Cameroon, Benin (Dahomey) in Africa and Peru, Mexico, and the United States in the Western Hemisphere.

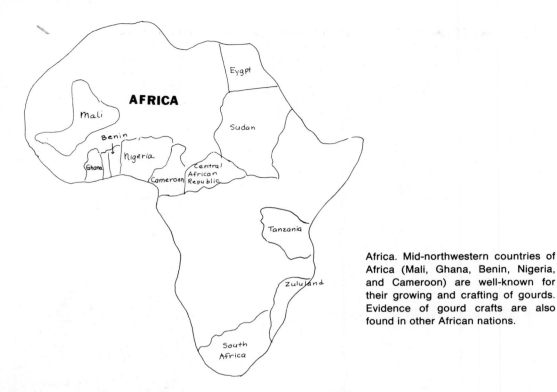

AFRICA

Africa. Mid-northwestern countries of Africa (Mali, Ghana, Benin, Nigeria, and Cameroon) are well-known for their growing and crafting of gourds. Evidence of gourd crafts are also found in other African nations.

AFRICA

African Gourd Decorating Techniques

PYRO-ENGRAVING	The burnt design is accomplished with a red hot leaf-shaped metal point set into a wooden handle. Several tools are heated in the fire at one time. Sometimes the outer skin of a thick-walled gourd is scraped away before it is burnt with a knife.
PRESSURE-ENGRAVING AND STAIN	The calabash is decorated by carving or incising a design with a steel point or a flat tip, shaped like a screwdriver. The incised decoration is stained with soot scraped from the bottom of pans, chalk, or oily Shee nut.
DYEING, THEN PRESSURE-ENGRAVING	The gourd is first dyed with natural dye, such as the paste of guinea cornstalk boiled with cottonseed oil, or else it is rubbed with a concoction of millet leaves. After the gourd has been dyed, the wall is engraved. The carving may expose the white layer beneath the skin or may be stained a dark color.
PYRO-ENGRAVING (BURNING), THEN DYEING	After the design is burnt on the gourd wall, the gourd is immersed in a hot dyebath or vice-versa. (The steps may be reversed.)
DYEING CARVED GREEN GOURDS	The gourd is carved while it is still green, then it is dyed. The resulting effect is that the carved areas absorb more dye and become darker than the tinted uncarved sections.

6

The beaded gourd with handle from Zululand is encased in an open network of seed beads that expose the gourd wall. The beads, slightly larger than those of the American Indians, vary in size and color (white, red, green, blue, gold, purple, and black). Courtesy, Eleanor Therien

Tanzanian gourd. Courtesy, British Museum

This decorated flask from Kenya has a carved stopper. Courtesy, British Museum

Pyro-engraved bowl from Mali. After the skin is scraped from the thick gourd wall, the line design is burned with a red-hot pointed metal-tipped tool. Courtesy, Carnegie Institute, Museum Shops

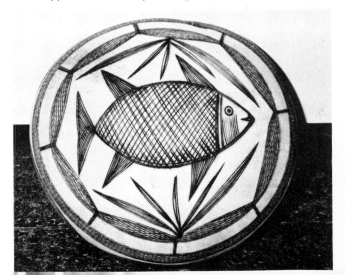

BEADING WITH BRIGHT COLORED SEED BEADS	Beaded encasements with geometric design cover the entire shape of the gourd.
EMBEDDING BEADS	Beads pressed into clay are placed into carved designs on the gourd.
EMBROIDERING	Sewn decoration or embroidery is applied through preworked holes in the gourd wall. Steel, brass, gold, or silver threads are used.
PLAITING THE GOURD WITH COCONUT FIBER	Coconut fiber is plaited to the exterior wall of the gourd.
WEAVING DECORATIVE COVERINGS AND BASES OVER GOURD CONTAINER	Decorative woven encasements cover various gourd containers.
PAINTING WITH BLACK ENAMEL, THEN CARVING	After brushing or dipping the gourd into black enamel paint, the gourd is carved exposing the light layer beneath.

African Gourd Art

The art of crafting and the ornamentation of gourds still thrives in countries of Africa, particularly in Western countries along the old camel route. Inhabitants of Mali, northern sections of the Ivory Coast, Ghana, Nigeria, and Benin still use and decorate gourds using the same methods as their ancestors. Gourd crafting extends from Cameroon, Central African Republic, Uganda, to Kenya and Tanzania, though the art is scattered as far south as the South African Republic.

A multitude of decorative techniques are mastered by the African people, each tribe specializing in one or two methods. Talented gourd artists are known for miles. As with other works of art, some artists are considered modern, while others in different tribes are labeled more traditional. Carvers do not see anything wrong with copying another artisan's work—copying is a form of flattery.

NIGERIA

The Nigerian calabash is used as a flask to hold water, milk, peanut oil, palm wine, as a bottle for shaking cream into butter, and as a measure for buying millet. The gourd also becomes a dipper for the well, a basin

A thick-shelled Nigerian gourd bowl with the outside skin removed has decorative geometrical openings cut through the gourd wall. The lid has a finger hole so that it can be lifted from the container.

Tula Baule calabash, a pyro-engraved hat, is from Nigeria. Courtesy, Dr. Barbara Rubin

for washing, and a dish for eating stews. Spoons are made by cutting narrow Bottle gourds lengthwise. Elaborately decorated calabash hats protect babies from the hot sun and rain. For centuries African witch doctors used gourds to store their medicine.

Some of the most beautifully decorated gourds in the world originate in Nigeria. Pyro-engraving (burning) or pressure-engraving (carving) is generally used for ornamentation. Straight or curvilinear designs -or a combination of both—are freely engraved over the surface. Some tribesmen have bold spaces between the design, while others embellish the gourd wall in a tight manner. After the gourds are carved, nut oil combined with soot scraped from the bottom of pans is rubbed over the gourd. The application deposits the contrasting dark soot in the engraved areas.

Some burnt gourds are cooked in a hot dyebath until the desired shade is obtained. Further patina is achieved from everyday handling in a smoky hut. Refer to chapter 5 for detailed illustrations and information on Nigerian gourd decorating methods.

GHANA

In Ghana patterns and abstract symbols are scratched into the gourd's exterior with an awl. Oily Shee nut, a black brown coloring agent, is rubbed into the engraved lines for a striking contrast with the gourd wall.

A less used technique of Ghana is sewing decoration to the gourd wall, actually a form of embroidery. Thin brass, steel, or gold wire is diagonally stitched through the calabash in long and winding pathways.

Adinkera ("good-bye" cloth), made by the Ashanti of Ghana, is a textile that is decorated with repeated motifs using gourd stamps. Small pieces of thick gourd wall are cut into different shapes, each having a significant meaning in the life of the people. The stamp is not larger than 3 inches in diameter because of the curvature of the gourd wall. A handle for the stamp is formed by attaching pieces of bamboo to the back of the stamp, then tieing them together at the top.

Dye for the Ashanti textile is made by adding Badie bark and iron slag to boiling water. After the components have cooked, the liquid is drained off. The dark mixture at the bottom of the pot is used for stamping the designs onto the fabric. White cotton material is then stretched over a board lined with a straw mat. A single stamp is pressed on the material row after row, until a rectangular section is complete. Different motifs, each having their rectangular area, are often repeated on one piece of cloth, with a solid unstamped space between. "Good-bye" cloth is worn when guests are leaving and at funeral services.

In Ghana, gourd stamps are used for printing textiles. Thick gourd shells are carved into various shapes that possess Ashanti names of historical or mystical significance. Gourd stamps, some with carved reliefs, have bamboo handles.

CAMEROON

At the present time Cameroon exports various objects made from gourds to different countries—calabash canisters, gourd pitchers with intricately designed woven encasements, and also gourd musical instruments such as the large bead-covered rattle. Some of Cameroon's gourd objects pictured in this book can be purchased at gift shops in museums and department stores.

A panel with an elongated animal is representative of Benin decoration on a bowl or lid.

BENIN (formerly called DAHOMEY)

Scraped and engraved gourds of the Bariba tribe are distinguished by their broad panel of distorted animals and figures. Bowls and lids are often divided by two or three horizontal bands. The spaces between contain rectangular panels of animals or figures, each elongated or distorted to occupy the space between the bands. The figures and animals are engraved inside the bars, zigzags, and crossbars. Plain and scraped areas and a few small engravings provide welcome negative space between the panels. Calabash gift boxes, some with carved love messages, were often presented by young men to girls of their fancy.

CENTRAL AND SOUTH AMERICA

For centuries the Central American countries, the West Indies, and many South American nations—Peru, Brazil, Bolivia, and Ecuador—used gourds as bowls, water flasks, sieves, and musical instruments. Today gourds are utilized as vessels mostly in the mountainous regions.

The importance of the gourd is truly demonstrated by the country of Haiti. Their paper money is called gourdes, the Spanish name for gourds. The use of gourdes as currency came about after the abolition of slavery. The Haitian people became dependent on wild produce, and gourds were necessary utensils. Chief Christophe declared that every green Lagenaria or ripening tree gourd in northern Haiti become the property of the state. Gourds were collected for the treasury by soldiers without objection from the peasants. Two hundred and twenty-seven thousand green gourds and calabashes were brought to Cap-Haïtien on high-piled carts.

"Dix-gourdes," or ten gourds. Gourd bills are used as a monetary exchange in the Republic of Haiti.

Christophe valued each gourd at twenty sous. When cultivators marketed ripe coffee beans at the capital, Christophe purchased the coffee using gourds as the medium of exchange. By this time the peasants accepted the gourds because they needed them badly.

Christophe in turn resold the coffee to European merchants for gold, enabling Haiti to circulate stable metal currency. From that time to the present the standard currency of Haiti was and is the gourde.

As far as ornamentation is concerned, gourd objects of Central and South America are undecorated and plain, or else they are often lacquered with designs or people in majestic settings. Many calabashes have carved or incised decorations that are either stained or left unstained. In Mexico forms of appliqué are applied to both the interior and exterior of the gourd.

The Maya of Guatemala decorate calabashes by blackening the gourd with fire smudge of pinewood. In Panama gourd containers are set in cocoa fiber holders. Central American sieves are often decorated with elegant carved designs.

Artisans of Peru create some of the most beautifully decorated and crafted gourds of this hemisphere, using the combined techniques of burning and carving with the natural coloring of the gourd.

PERU

Peruvian Decorating Techniques

Burning with acid applied with a stick.

Carving using pointed tool or screwdriver.

Carving and staining with charcoal paste from burnt grass.

Dyeing and stained carving.

Inlaying with turquoise and silver.

Burning with stick of eucalyptus and carving.

Painting the gourd with bright colors.

The ornamentation of the *mati*, the popular name for gourd, is a Peruvian art that predates pottery and continues to the present time. Throughout history two types of characteristic gourds were common in Peru: the Porongo and the Poto. The Porongo is a Bottle gourd with a ball base and a narrow neck at the stem end. It was used as a container for water, fermented cider, milk, and honey. The round gourd Poto is level at the top and bottom. The Poto was used as a sugar bowl, drinking cup, basket, and washing trough. Spoons were made from the long thin-necked Chucula.

The gourd on a pedestal is a representation of a Peruvian woman in her native Indian costume. The gourd is masterfully carved and burned so that four shades of color appear on the surface: black and brown from burning and shading, white lines from carving, plus the natural color of the gourd wall. Courtesy, Raquel's Collection

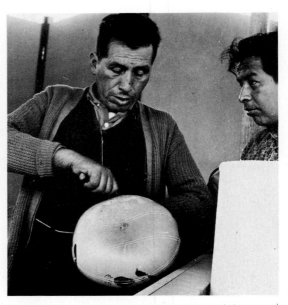

The Peruvian artisan carves the surface of the gourd with a screwdriver-shaped tool called a burin. Courtesy, Museo Nacional de la Cultura Peruana. Photographed by Seno Wilfredo Loaza

The earliest decorated gourds of Peru and this hemisphere were excavated at the preceramic site in Huaca Prieta, Peru. Using the carbon dating method, the objects dated back to about 2,500 B.C. One gourd found in this excavation was carved with stylized fish, game, figures, and faces. Other early gourds were decorated by burning their walls with acid.

During the Pre-Columbian era in the early history of Peru, Incas filled nets with gourds to make rafts for crossing rivers. The Incas also used netted gourds for fishing buoys as evidenced at the excavated site in Huaca Prieta. In addition, gourds were fashioned into cribs for babies, objects used at religious ceremonies, and musical instruments.

Scenes portraying the life and events of the times embellished the gourds. Spanish and Arabic elements were introduced into the picturesque designs covering the gourds; many diversified techniques of decorating became prevalent. In Huanta, artisans carved sugar bowls with a burin, an implement having a screwdriver-shaped tip. The incised background was filled with charcoal paste, which contrasted with the natural coloring of the gourd wall. The most exquisite combination of carving and burning the surface of the gourd with a piece of eucalyptus wood was developed. Other less common techniques were inlaying with silver or turquoise and painting. The decorated calabashes were bartered at fairs and were used as containers for wine, cider, liquor, and honey.

During the era of the Republic, after Peruvian independence, ornamentation of the gourd reached its purest expression. Elaborately carved or burnt scenes typified all that was important in Peruvian life. A multitude of scenes were carved or burnt at various levels over the entire surface of the gourd. Or else a lifelike scene was contained between decorative borders at the top and bottom of the calabash. The elevation of gourd art during the nineteenth century promoted the decorated gourd to what is now called a "popular" art.

Right:
This gourd, burned with acid, is from the province of Pacasmayo. Courtesy, Museo Nacional de la Cultura Peruana. Photographed by Seno Wilfredo Loaza
Below:
The gourd bowl from Lambayeque in northern Peru has a simple design burned with acid, which is applied with a stick. Twentieth century. Courtesy, Museo Nacional de la Cultura Peruana. Photographed by Seno Wilfredo Loaza

The glory of the new era of the Republic of Peru is evidenced by this historical decorated gourd box from Ayacucho. The elegant design, done in 1848, is accomplished by burning and carving. Spanish inscriptions are carved in borders near the top and bottom of the gourd. Courtesy, Museo Nacional de la Cultura Peruana. Photographed by Seno Wilfredo Loaza

The Porongo gourd from Ayacucho is burned with two scenes depicting the life of the people. The scenic panels, one on top of the other, are separated by a plain border. Courtesy, Museo Nacional de la Cultura Peruana. Photographed by Seno Wilfredo Loaza

The continuous burnt scene shows groups of people in the foreground with buildings in the back. This twentieth-century gourd is from the vicinity of Ayacucho. Courtesy, Museo Nacional de la Cultura Peruana. Photographed by Seno Wilfredo Loaza

The active centers of the Republic era continue on the north coast states of Lambayeque and Piura, in the mountains of Junín, and in the states of Ayacucho and Huancavelica. Each region retains its own method for decorating gourds—Lambayeque and Junín continue to burn with a stick or with acid. Particularly in Ayacucho and in Huancavelica, gourd decoration still depicts the life of the people.

Presently artisans continue to sell their work at fairs where neighboring countries participate. Decorated calabashes are bought by tourists and traded with other countries. In Peru gourds have mostly become decorative objects admired for their beauty, but there are a few traditional regions where gourds are still being used for utilitarian purposes.

MEXICO

Methods of Decorating Gourds

Lacquering using special techniques.

Adorning the gourd wall with colored yarns.

Applying bead designs to the interior of vessels.

Carving.

Lacquerware techniques originated in Mexican preconquest times before the arrival of the Spanish. One method is to first lacquer the gourd with a dark color. After this background color is applied, a design is cut through the lacquer. Colored pigments are then rubbed into the openings of the paint with the palm of the hand.

Another lacquering technique involves two coats of lacquer. The initial coat of paint is usually dark (usually black) for the background. After the second coat is applied, a design is incised with a thorn attached to a feather. The resulting effect is a design that stands out from the background. It is often modeled to form a texture that produces fine shadows. The entire process is described in detail in chapter 6.

Appliqué decorating methods are used by the Huichol women of mountainous San Andres. Bottle gourds are painted with rows of colored yarns. Stylized animals and people are created by adhering curved rows of yarn to the gourd wall with melted beeswax. Solid figures are surrounded by whole adjacent areas of contrasting colored yarn.

Huichol women also apply bead decoration to the interior walls of calabash bowls. Representations of plants, animals, and people are confined by decorative borders. They are created by the meticulous placement of hundreds of seed beads in a mosaiclike fashion. Bright royal colored beads are partially embedded in the process.

In Mexico, gourds are carved with no additional stain or added coloring. Meaningful allover designs, often of religious significance, cover the exterior surface of the gourd. An eagle is a common motif. The only coloring is a starchy red clay, which is used to finish the thin interior wall.

The intricately carved Mexican gourd bowl with a Spanish inscription is a product of the OAY coast. The carved areas are unstained. Courtesy, Mexican Folk Art Annex

Huichol seed bead bowl. The stylized decoration is made by setting hundreds of colored seed beads, one by one, in a coat of warm beeswax on the inner gourd wall. Courtesy, Carnegie Institute, Museum Shops

UNITED STATES

Methods of Decorating Gourds

* Carving with small hand wood-carving implements, then staining. Carving with electrical tools.

* Painting with oils, enamels, or acrylics.

* Burning with electric wood burner.

Antiquing with paints and stains used for wood.

* These techniques are the ones most commonly practiced in the United States.

Sculpturing with glues, fine nails, Sculptamold ®.

Applying decoupage material.

Batiking with leather dyes.

Coloring with vegetable dyes.

Applying commercial wood stains.

Appliquéing yarns, gourd seeds, macramé, etc.

Providing mechanical movements for toys, clocks, and scenes.

Using felt-tip markers with permanent colors.

Decorating with India ink.

Gold leafing.

Before the colonization of North America, the Southwest Indians developed an entire line of necessities and treasures from the Lagenaria. Their gourd objects included water bottles, toys, storage containers, ladles, spoons, funnels, cornmeal sifters, measures, salt containers, seed holders, food bowls, egg holders, baskets, net line and swimming floats, musical instruments (rattles), and masks for ceremonial dances.

Many Indian tribes throughout the North American continent made gourd containers, dippers, dance and medicine rattles, and masks. Gourd rattles are found as far north as the Iroquois in Canada. Tribes known to have utilized gourds are the Apache, Comanche, Wichita, and Shawnee of Oklahoma. The Cherokee in North Carolina created masks for the Booger dance-one, a clown with a long nose trimmed with fox fur. A decorative painted mask representing a bear clan was used for their New Year's ceremony.

In the West the Hopi also created ceremonial masks. The chief, kachina, in the kiva ceremonies of the Hopi carried calabash water containers in nets. The Pueblo Indians of New Mexico placed a gourd containing prayer plumes on the floor of the house where the snake dance was performed.

In colonial times the narrow Club gourd was used by the colonists to store grain and to carry seeds. It was fashioned with an opening and leather thong handle at one end. New England gourd water dippers were of such value that they were bequeathed in wills.

Generally, the Lagenaria has not been used for utilitarian purposes in the United States for many years, because of the availability of mass-produced ceramic and metal products. There has been a lack of information on the subject of Hardshelled gourds. Nevertheless, a loyal minority of gourdists from almost every state in the union continue to receive pleasure from growing and crafting Lagenaria.

From the 1940s to the 1950s Harold Pearson of El Monte, California, devoted forty acres to the growing of gourds. He created a market for gourd crafts, specializing in decorated fruit baskets, candy containers, Ramona charm strings, and much more.

Marvin Johnson is the notable gourd farmer through the 1960's to the 1980's. On his North Carolina estate he raises exotic gourds -- from the African Wine Kettle to the Corsican Tobacco Box -- with seeds from all over the world. To produce true strains, he plants seeds of each type with a wooded area between. Currently, Mr. Johnson is working with the Department of Agriculture at North Carolina University to develop a Lagenaria seed that will produce a football.

The first important gourd association in the United States was the New England Gourd Society begun in 1936. In 1942 the New England Gourd Society then became incorporated as the Gourd Society of America. This organization, active during the 1960's, published a periodical called *The Gourd Seed.* Members of the association published their collective information on the growing and crafting of gourds in the book *Gourds: Their Culture and Craft.* Their ethnological series, written by certain members, included *Gourd Growers of the South Seas* by Ernst Dodge, *Gourds of the South Western Indians* by Frank Speck, and *Gourds in Folk Literature* by Eddie W. Wilson.

Artistic display exhibited at the Ohio Gourd Show. Glenn Swenson

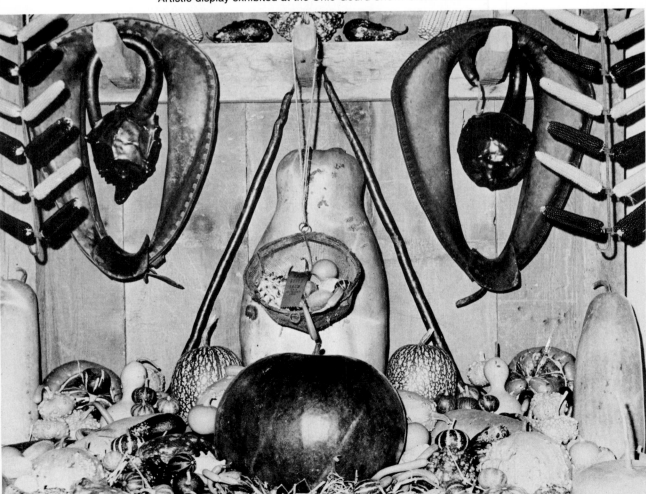

The batiked basket with lid is made using the wax-resist process of employing leather dyes. Carolyn Mordecai

African gourd rattle from Cameroon. Beads are strung onto a loosely fitted net that covers the gourd wall. When the gourd is shaken, the rattling sound is produced externally. Courtesy, Carnegie Institute, Museum Shops

The abstract design on the gourd lamp is burned with a propane torch, then carved, exposing the white lining of the natural gourd wall. Carolyn Mordecai

Ornamental gourd wreath. A woven mat fringed with silky fibers of Manila rope features Apple and Pear gourds and a Crown of Thorns over loops of patchwork ribbon. Carolyn Mordecai

International bowl. The figures representing each country are outlined by a wood burner, then filled with light and dark areas of mahogany stain. Carolyn Mordecai

The self-portrait of Minnie Black is sculpted from various types of Lagenaria and Ornamental gourds. Courtesy, Minnie Black

Swedish calabashes are decorated with burnt designs using a soldering copper. Courtesy, John Kraft

The Nut Hut is a canister-shaped gourd painted with earth colors and adorned with nuts. The gourd canister is used to store the family's supply of nuts.

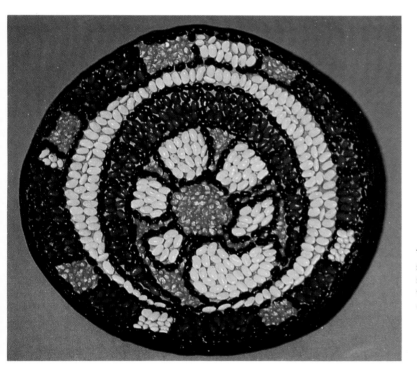

The inside wall of the organic seed platter is covered with an abstract design made from red, white, and black beans and yellow corn. Carolyn Mordecai

The Huichol seed bead bowl from San Andres, Mexico, is decorated with hundreds of seed beads embedded in beeswax. Courtesy, Mexican Folk Art Annex

The carved and painted free-form sculpture is made from shapely Bottle and Penguin Lagenaria and Pear-shaped Ornamental gourds. Carolyn Mordecai

Artistic display of Ornamental and Lagenaria gourds. Courtesy, Wilda Vogelhuber

The lacquered box with a fine sculpted design is representative of Olina work, from Mexico. Courtesy, Mexican Folk Art Annex

The Peruvian Indian woman is carved with a burin, a screwdriver-shaped tool, and burned in with a heated piece of eucalyptus wood. Courtesy, Raquel's Collection

Pyro-engraved bowl by Lami of Kwaya, Nigeria. Courtesy, Dr. Barbara Rubin. Photograph by Larry DuPont

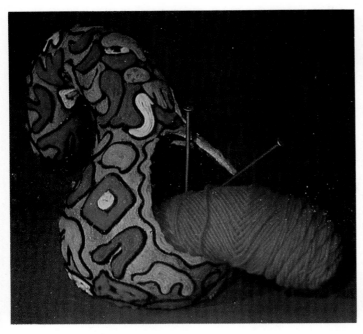

The yarn-painted tote is a crooked-necked gourd designed to store yarn. Carolyn Mordecai

Hanging-gourd sculpture. Mahogany-painted Lagenarias are attached with multicolored coil-woven cylinders. Long strands of rope are threaded in and out of the gourds to establish lines. Carolyn Mordecai

The Zucca gourd grandfather clock has a long swinging Dipper gourd pendulum. Courtesy, Eugene Deardorff

The soft-sculptured vase has three coil-woven spouts attached to the rim of a warty Lagenaria bowl. Carolyn Mordecai

Gourd pitcher from Cameroon. The gourd rests inside an intricately woven base with handle. Courtesy, Carnegie Institute, Museum Shops

Display of Ornamental spoon gourds.

Carved and painted Peruvian gourd. Courtesy, Museum of Marvin Johnson

Pyro-engraved (burnt) gourd from Mali. The skin is scraped from the gourd wall, and a line design is burned with a red-hot, pointed, metal-tipped tool. Courtesy, Carnegie Institute, Museum Shops

The Peruvian carved and burnt sugar bowl is embellished with a scenic panel depicting the everyday life of the people. Courtesy, Sergio Carvajal, Precolumbian Jewels, Inc.

The commemorative gourd for the United States bicentennial was carved by Dr. Leslie Miller of Ohio. Courtesy, Dr. Leslie Miller

The geometrically carved and stained gourd features stars and triangles. Dr. Leslie Miller

When the Ohio members took over the New England Gourd Society in 1971, it was incorporated as the American Gourd Society. The American Gourd Society, Inc. is the present society covering the entire United States. Their quarterly (Winter, Spring, Summer, Fall) publication *The Gourd,* Ted Modrowski Editor, covers news articles and photography about history, growing, and crafting gourds. Featured also are special exhibits, news from other gourd clubs, letters from members, information about knowledgeable friends or organizations and classifieds of gourd seeds and ready-grown gourds. Address correspondence to the American Gourd Society, Inc., P.O. Box 274, Mount Gilead, Ohio 43338.

Affiliated Gourd associations in different states are the Alpha Chapter - Gourd Village Garden Club in Cary, North Carolina; the Beta Chapter - Ohio Gourd Society in Mt. Gilead, Ohio; Gamma Chapter in Phoenix, Arizona; and the Delta Chapter - New River Valley Gourd Society in Christiansburg, Virginia are the backbone of the American Gourd Society. The American Gourd Society holds an annual meeting in July at the Mt. Gilead headquarters. Their president is now Wilda M. Vogelhuber.

The Ohio Gourd Society sponsors the largest gourd raising and crafting competition in the country on the fairgrounds of Mt. Gilead in Ohio. O.C. Stevens, honorary chairman, gourd raiser, lecturer, and judge has been chairman of the show during its entire existence from 1952 to the present. John Stevens is now active chairman with the help of many dedicated members. At the two-day competition, freshly harvested Ornamentals and Lagenarias are evaluated. Cultural perfection, quality, maturity, and coloring of all types are judged and admired. Artistic fresh gourd displays of the current season line the buildings' walls. A competition for the largest Lagenarias is completed after each gourd is measured and weighed.

Craft categories exhibited include jewelry, charm rings, artistic gourds, fresh and dried arrangements, gourd seed crafts, hanging baskets, bowls, dolls, holiday decor, birdhouses and feeders, pitchers, gourd animals, dippers, lamps, hats, and musical instruments. A few of the highlights of the exhibit are the mechanical and electrical gourd displays with movable parts and lights. Out-of-state exhibitors are encouraged to attend the show and bring their gourds and crafts for the competition.

The decorated gourds at the show and throughout the United States are usually burned with an electrical wood burner, carved and stained, or painted with a design. Animals, people, and sculpture are put together using modern adhesives. Hand and electrical carving tools, purchased at crafts or hardware stores, are used for convenience and to obtain special effects.

Expert American gourd artists are Larue Stith of Ohio who uses electrical wood burners to produce museum quality work, Dr. Leslie Miller, a mathematics professor in Ohio, who is known for carving and staining perfect geometric designs, and Minnie Black of Kentucky who creates true-to-life sculpture of animals and people.

Over the years most museums of art and anthropology usually have had calabashes well hidden in their collections, though Indian gourds are shown in some museums of the Southwest. However, there are a few museums and small private collections that specialize in gourds. The private museum of Marvin Johnson in Fuquay Varina, North Carolina, houses the work of gourd artists from the United States and Central and South America. Mrs. Minnie Black of East Bernstadt, Kentucky, displays her exceptional lifelike sculpted people and animals in her own museum. Gourd objects from the New England area and from foreign countries are exhibited at the Unitarian Church in East Bridgewater, Massachusetts.

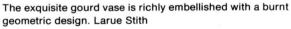

The exquisite gourd vase is richly embellished with a burnt geometric design. Larue Stith

Spirit of '76. Democratic donkey and Republican elephant shaking hands. Courtesy of Ralph Schneider

The pioneer wagon and oxen, approximately 3 feet in length, is made almost entirely from Lagenaria and Ornamental gourds, except for the cover on the wagon and a few strips of leather. Minnie Black

The Luffa gourd bath sponge is sold with cosmetics in large department stores. Kaufmanns

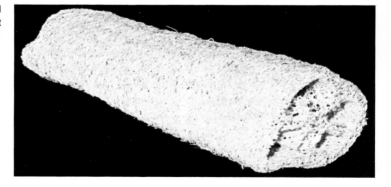

The long green cylindrical Luffa gourd, sometimes called a vegetable sponge or dishrag gourd, has a fibrous tightly woven spongelike material on the inside. The fruit grows from 12 to 24 inches long on vines climbing from 10 to 15 feet. When the ripened Luffas are immersed in water, the outer wall disintegrates. Then the sponges are bleached and dried in the sun. The Luffa sponge is often used for bathing or even as a pot scraper. Commercially, it is grown in Japan for mats, sandals, and pillow stuffing. Though Luffas are thought to have originated in tropical Asia, they can be grown in tropical and temperate areas of the United States. Immature Luffas are delicious cooked like summer squash.

Lagenaria have been used in many different countries as the following:

Containers

Boxes to nest barnyard fowl
Birdhouses, feeders, cages
Doghouses
Cookie jars
Flower baskets
Sewing baskets
Purses
Salt and pepper shakers
Popcorn bowls
Table planters
Cornucopias
Grain storage baskets
Match holders
Cigarette and pipe holders
Wastebaskets

Bath powder containers
Medicine jars
Fruit bowls
Hanging baskets
Vases
"Leave-a-Note" bowls
Flasks for water, oil, honey, wine
Gunpowder holders
Seed containers
Tobacco boxes
Jewelry boxes
Money holders
Wash basins
Food preservers
Cribs for babies

Utensils

Spoons, scoops, ladles
Measures
Strainers, sieves
Funnels

Napkin holders
Pipes
Darning balls

Small Gourd Ornaments

Christmas tree decorations
Ornaments for wreaths and
    door decorations
Components of crafted flowers
Small items in plaques
Animal novelties

Embellishment in floral design
    and centerpieces
Charm strings
Jewelry
Hats
Neckerchief slides

Others

Rafts
Fishing floats
Doorbells
Humming tops
Lamp bases
Heads for puppets
Masks
Figures of animals and people

Modern sculptures
Musical instruments—rattles,
    guiro, drums, flutes, whistles,
    sitars, lutes, guitars, violins,
    marimbas, harps
Dollhouses
Decorated whole gourds for
    household decoration

The Three Musketeers are sculpted from Luffa gourd sponges. The fibrous material is painted with appropriate colors. Ralph Schneider

SPIRIT OF 1776

The realistic eagle is made from the fibrous material of the Luffa gourd. Minnie Black

Though many gourds are crafted for utilitarian purposes, these beautifully carved gourds are used solely as decoration. Dr. Leslie Miller. Courtesy, Marvin Johnson

25

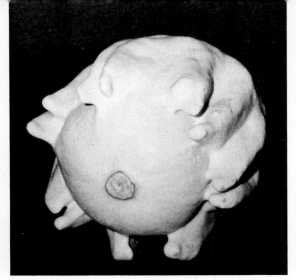

The elegant off-white ten-fingered Ornamental gourd is called the Crown of Thorns, Holy Crown, or Ten Commandments gourd.

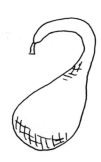

Ornamental gourds. Nest Egg, Apple, Orange, Pear *(top row)*. Bell, Spoon *(bottom row)*.

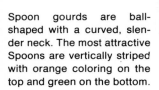

Spoon gourds are ball-shaped with a curved, slender neck. The most attractive Spoons are vertically striped with orange coloring on the top and green on the bottom.

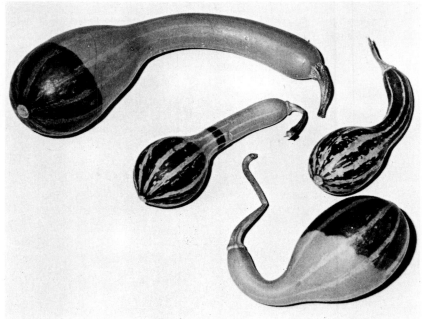

Ornamental Gourds

Ornamental gourds are the brilliantly colored small fruited gourds that provide seasonal decoration at harvesttime. Their coloring ranges from yellow gold to orange, pale green to forest green, and off-white. The shapely fruits may have plain or beautifully patterned, warty, or smooth surfaces. Compared to the Lagenaria, Ornamentals are much smaller and have a thicker, soft shell, resembling that of a pumpkin or squash. Ornamentals are more perishable than Lagenarias. Many disintegrate within a few months, but those ripe Ornamentals that dry well can be used for crafts purposes.

Seed growers have developed distinctive shapes and coloring of Ornamental gourds over the years by isolating growing areas for each type. A particular kind of gourd receives its name from its shape:

Miniature Bottle

Nest Egg—white, shaped like an egg

Orange, Mock Orange—has shape and coloring of an orange

Pears

    White Pear—formerly used as a darning ball

    Striped Pear—yellow and green stripes

    Bicolored Pear—handle has yellow stripes; the lower half is green with dark stripes

Spoon—ball-shaped end with long curved slender neck, often yellow or orange striped on top with green on the bottom

Holy Crown, Crown of Thorns, Ten Commandments Gourd, or Finger Gourd—off-white with ten fingers extending up from the side of the gourd

Apple—Light yellow to white, round or ribbed, smooth or warty

Bell—Yellow, yellow with irregular patches of green, slightly ridged

Big Bell—4 to 6 inches, slightly warty, dark green or creamy white

Depressa Striata—flat, ridged, odd-shaped

Raising Ornamental Gourds

Ornamentals are easy to cultivate and thrive where squash and pumpkins grow well. The best location for growing gourd plants is in rich, well-drained mounds of soil under full sunlight. For vigorous growth and greater production, place a shovelful of well-rotted manure under the planting surface of each mound. The seeds that sprout in the original top soil will form roots which receive nutrients from the rotted manure beneath. Another way to enrich the soil is by working fertilizer around the edge of each mound where it will not touch the seeds. Nitrogen fertilizer is used only for initial planting. If nitrogen fertilizer is used later, the fertilizer will encourage vines instead of gourds to grow.

Plant 5–6 seeds in each mound after the danger of frost has passed. Cover each seed with fine soil, then press down. After the seeds sprout, allow them to grow into small plants. Then thin each hill down to two or three of the strongest plants as long as they are well separated from each other.

If the gourd vines are to grow over the ground, six to eight feet of space is needed between each mound. It is better to raise the gourds off the ground so that they will be relatively uniform in color and escape blemishes. Gourd plants may be trained over an arbor, arched chicken wire, or up a trellis, stone wall, or wooden fence. Plastic sheets may be used to protect gourds that touch the ground.

As the viny, broad-leafed plants grow, you will notice yellow or orange flowers that open during daylight hours for pollination. Ornamentals will not pollinate with other members of the Cucurbitaceae family—cucumbers or squash. However, different kinds of Ornamentals will cross-pollinate if planted together. If pure stocks are desired, the types should be widely separated when the seeds are planted.

To care for your Ornamentals, simply water or irrigate the plants during dry spells. As the gourds reach their full size, extra watering is withheld so that they will ripen before the first frost.

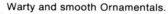

Warty and smooth Ornamentals.

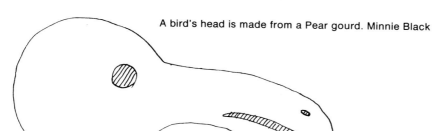

A bird's head is made from a Pear gourd. Minnie Black

The tea ball is fashioned by drilling small holes through one end of a Nest Egg gourd. An opening is cut at the top for placing the tea leaves inside. The ball is held by a dipping string placed through holes near the opening of the gourd and through the cap. Designed by Eileen and Tom Holt. Illustrated by Gary Feuerstein

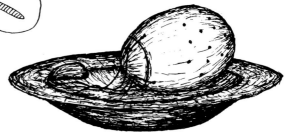

The pipe is a Pear Ornamental with an inverted metal saltshaker top inserted into the round opening in the ball of the gourd. Designed by Craig Lewis. Illustrated by Gary Feuerstein

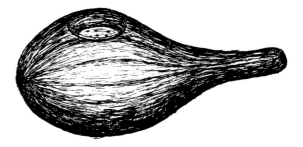

The realistic reptile is made from warty Ornamentals. Minnie Black

Star gourd.

Pencil holder. The bottom gourd is weighted so that the pencil holder will not tip over. Minnie Black

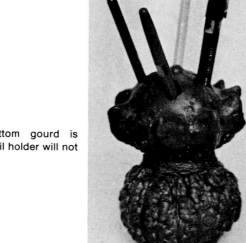

The panoramic Christmas ornament is a Pear gourd with an opening to view the winter scene. Miniature animals for the inside may be carved or molded from sculptural materials or homemade clays (bread or play dough). Tiny figures may also be purchased at craft stores. Karen Feuerstein. Illustrated by Gary Feuerstein

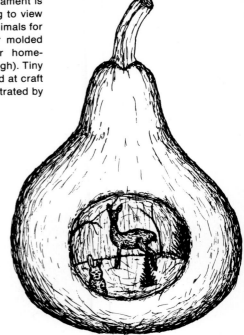

The decoupaged place-setting accompaniment has a print applied to its surface with Mod Podge. The entire gourd and print is given a final coat of Mod Podge with a soft brush.

Harvesting Ornamental Gourds

Ornamentals take approximately 130 days to mature. They are ready for harvesting when they become hard to the touch and when their stems become dry and brown. The gourds should be harvested before the first frost, but they must absolutely be harvested after the initial freeze. If they are subject to three or four repeated frosts, the cold will badly affect their keeping qualities.

To cut gourds from the vine, remove them with a clipper, leaving at least one inch or more of stem on the fruit. Handle the gourd carefully to avoid bruising. Bruised spots often can be a source of rotting, which will ruin the entire fruit. Save your best gourds for seeds to be planted the following year.

Preserving Ornamental Gourds

Presently, there is no scientific method for permanently preserving the beautiful coloring of Ornamental gourds. Most lose their color within six months, though orange gourds usually retain their color longer—large warties up to two years.

Fresh Ornamentals may be preserved for several months by wiping them with a nonbleaching disinfectant, such as Lysol, a solution of vinegar and water, or two tablespoons of borax mixed with a quart of water. Then polish the fresh gourd with a colorless paste wax for wooden floors or with car wax. Shellac and varnish, occasionally used, give the gourds a glossy appearance.

A natural woven basket provides a neutral color that blends with the bright and colorful Ornamental gourds.

Display of Lagenaria and Ornamental gourds. Glenn Swenson

Smaller types of mature Ornamentals will retain their coloring up to two years or more by boiling them in a thick mixture of borax and water for at least fifteen minutes. When finished, the gourds are removed and placed in wire baskets or netting to expose them to the air. After they dry—at least several weeks—they are washed in warm water. Finally, the dry gourds are waxed, then polished.

Displaying Fresh Gourds

The best gourds for exhibiting are free from blemishes and discoloring. Generally, they are grown off the ground on a fence, chicken wire, or trellis. The gourds should be cut from the vines leaving their stems intact. Ornamentals may be arranged without crowding in a neutral or natural colored basket, tray, wooden bowl, or breakfront. Brightly colored containers usually distract from their brilliance.

31

Stick the needle holder near the bottom edge of the basket with florist's clay.

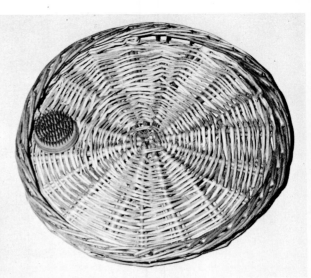

"Harvesttime" is a brightly colored seasonal arrangement created from nature's bounty: fresh Ornamental gourds, cornstalks, cardone puffs, lotus pods in a low-walled woven basket.

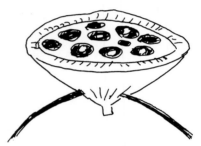

Predrill two holes on the bottom of the lotus pod. A small hole on each side of the pod's base can be drilled with an electric drill with a fine bit or with a sharp pointed tool. After drilling, insert a 12-inch length of 24–26-gauge wire through the holes.

Wire the stems of the following plant materials together to form a lengthy bunch: cornstalks, cattails, lotus pods (use wire stems), and cardone puffs. These materials, when standing upright, should be two and a half times the width of the container. Cut off longer stems with clippers. Then wind masking tape over the wired stems from top to bottom so that the mechanics are not exposed and the plant stems are tightly secured.

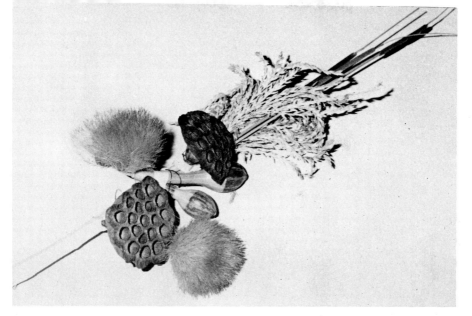

After sticking a wad of florist's clay onto the corner of the mat, push a needle holder into the clay. Insert the gathering of stem materials vertically over the needle holder. Finally, arrange the Ornamental gourds from the base of the gathering into a simple invisible curved line, which leads out the front of the mat.

Curing Ornamental Gourds for Display or for Craft Purposes

Ornamentals that often dry to a natural thin dull finish are the Crown of Thorns, Pears, Apples, Eggs, Orange, Warties, and sometimes Spoons. If the gourds are mature when they are picked, they will usually dry well. As the gourds dry, their colors will fade, and they will become covered with mold or crust. Many people unknowingly throw the gourds away at that time because of their undesirable appearance, never knowing the beauty that lies beneath. After curing or drying, they need only a good cleaning to expose their smooth, natural surface.

To cure Ornamentals, wipe them with one of the solutions used to preserve gourds—the borax solution or the nonbleaching disinfectant. It is not necessary to wax, shellac, or varnish gourds to be used for crafts purposes until you know what you will be making with them. Dry the Ornamentals on a rack, allowing the air to circulate around each gourd. This curing process is best accomplished where the humidity is low. While drying, occasionally turn each gourd exposing all surfaces to the air.

Some craftspeople drill holes in each end to facilitate drying. Others believe that piercing holes in Ornamental gourds subjects them to disease. Anyway, they will eventually dry without being pierced. Gourds that disintegrate or shrivel while drying can be discarded. The gourds that dry properly will have a thin, solid shell. They will be light in weight and their seeds will rattle.

The mold and crust can be removed from the gourds under warm water with a dull knife and a steel wool pad. After cleaning, the gourds are then dried with a soft rag. Beautiful creamy shells will be the wonderful results of your cleaning efforts.

33

Place-setting accompaniment. The guest's name and floral decoration is drawn over the gourd with colored felt-tipped markers.

The fine line design on the surface of the cured Apple gourd is drawn with an artist's drafting pen and India ink. (The pen is pictured in chapter 5.) Carolyn Mordecai

Ornamentals may be left outside on a trellis to freeze in cold areas of the country. When spring arrives, the skin loosens and cleaning is easy. The designs created by the mold will be missing. Incidentally, the seeds from gourds that freeze outside during the winter will not germinate as well as the seeds brought indoors.

Finishes

Cleaned and cured unwaxed Ornamentals can be first sanded, then polished using a paste floor wax for wood. The gourds may be also dyed to a transparent tint by immersing them in a hot concentrated dyebath composed of clothing dye and boiling water. Deeper coloring may be obtained by brushing or dipping the gourds into leather dyes.

Ornamentals can be darkened with wood stains, varnished or painted various colors with oil paints, acrylics, and lacquer. Paints are applied with a brush, by spraying or dipping. Besides painting designs with a fine brush, gourds can be decorated with an electric woodburning tool.

The small shapely Ornamentals make fine extremities for animals, heads for dolls, unusual jewelry, small kitchen utensils, and fascinating decorations for wreaths, swags, and holiday ornaments.

Ornamental Gourd Wreath

An effective gourd wreath has an abundance of colorful materials that contrast with the neutral coloring of cured Ornamental gourds. A variety of smooth and textured materials, seasonal props, ribbons and multi-ply yarn, are available from many sources—florists, department and grocery stores, arts and craft shops, and mail-order firms. Plant materials may be found in the countryside or may be purposely planted in your own backyard.

WREATH BASES

To make a gourd wreath for the home or office, choose the size of the wreath base to fit the intended space. The type of wreath base depends on your personal preference. The most common base for attaching materials is the three-dimensional circular four-wired frame. In order to keep objects wired to this frame from slipping, prewrap the wires of the frame with floral tape. Then secure objects to the frame with 24- or 26-gauge wire, also wrapped with tape. The additional time and effort spent on wrapping endeavor will provide you with a substantial wreath that lasts for years.

Secondly, there are white or green Styrofoam rounds that can be purchased in a crafts shop or all-purpose department store. Styrofoam provides an adequate base for lightweight materials. It may be wound with dark green or brown florist's tape so that the white or green background color will not show through after the objects are inserted. Strong-stemmed materials can be pushed directly into the Styrofoam. Special picks may be purchased at the florist's for inserting more difficult objects.

A straw base is appropriate for both fresh and dried material. The natural stems or wire stems are simply pushed into the straw. Modern wreaths often expose the straw frame as part of the design.

The plywood circle, painted a dark color, can be a base for a gourd wreath when holes are predrilled through the wood for attaching the objects. Vines, such as wisteria or grape, may be worked together to make a natural "no-cost" wreath base. Other backings originating from nature are woven mats or low-walled woven containers, which are often imported from foreign countries.

ORNAMENTATION OF A GOURD WREATH

Decorative materials that may be used in a gourd wreath are dried flowers, glycerined foliage, nuts, pods, cones, weeds, and grasses. Others include handcrafted flowers and various types of plain or patterned ribbons, yarns, and burlap.

Cones

To make flowerlets from pinecones, soak the cones in water. After their petals have closed, lay the cones on their sides and saw the slices vertically. When each slice is dry, the petals will open to form flowers. Remove the damaged petals. Another method for making flowerlets is to cut cross-segments of open cones with heavy clippers.

Nuts

Bake nuts in an oven set at 250 degrees for one hour to prevent insect infestation. Drill straight through nuts, acorns, eucalyptus pods, and large seeds with an electric drill having a one-sixteenth-inch bit. Insert 24- 26-gauge florist's wire through the hole. Usually nuts and other small ornaments are wired into bunches, then taped before attaching them to the wreath frame.

If you do not want to drill holes through the nuts or pods, cover each object with Saran or other plastic wrap. Shrink the wrap over each nut under hot water and tie the bunched ends of the wrap together with fine wire. Another optional covering is stretch netting, which can be purchased at the fabric store, but it is rather expensive.

GENERAL DIRECTIONS FOR WREATH MAKING

The Motif

A motif is a center of attraction, a combination of important decorative materials attached to the wreath base. On a small or large

A single motif may be placed at the base of the wreath or off to one side. When two motifs are used, one is attached to the top and the other to the bottom of the frame. Three motifs are equally spaced to form an equilateral triangle.

wreath the single motif is usually placed on the bottom or occasionally off to one side. Larger wreaths can support two or three motifs. The wreath with two motifs has one at the top and the other at the bottom. A wreath having three motifs has each attached in triangular fashion at equal intervals.

Ornamental gourds, particularly the larger ones, are wired separately to the frame. But other objects forming the motif are secured in bunches, like corsages, before they are attached. A motif is often comprised of as many as two or three "corsages." To form a corsage, gather the plant materials, graduating in size from small to large. Wire, then wind the stems together with florist's tape. The gathering, or corsage, should be composed of alternating smooth and textured materials with a contrast of color in adjacent materials. Well-made corsages are easy to attach to the frame and give the wreath lasting qualities, which will provide for years of enjoyment.

The Hanging Device

The hanging loop attached to the back of the wreath can be a doubled fourteen- to sixteen-inch 24-gauge wire or else one strong plyable wire. It is best to wind the wires with florist's tape before making the loop so that the hanging device will not scratch a door or wall. Use the diagram directions to form the loop:

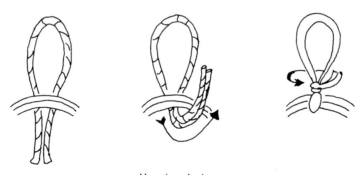

Hanging device.

Storing the Wreath

To store a wreath, suspend it from a hook on the top of a clothes hanger. Cut a small hole midway in the crease of a large-size garbage bag or cleaner bag. Fit the bag over the wreath, inserting the hook of the hanger through the hole.

Ornamental gourd wreath. The gourd wreath is a lovely, warm hanging over a fireplace of a dark paneled room. The base is a round woven mat, its looped edges fringed with silky fibers of Manila rope. Over the knotted fringe is a circle of looped patchwork ribbon. The motif at the bottom starts in the center with the Crown of Thorns gourd, flanked by loops of ribbon. The focal point is enhanced on each side by ears of strawberry and miniature Ornamental corn. Carolyn Mordecai

Ornamental Gourd Wreath

If you plan to make a similar gourd wreath, it is not necessary to have the same materials pictured here as ornamentation. You may substitute other plant materials and ribbon. Instead of using small pinecones for the inner circle, you may attach pinecone flowerlets or sweet gum balls. Though patchwork ribbon is looped around the wreath in the photograph, you may find checked, plaid, flowered, or plain ribbon more suitable for your scheme. Save money by cutting extra fabric into strips of ribbon with pinking sheers. If the material is soft, soak it in Elmer's glue and water; let it dry. Then iron the fabric ribbon with a steam iron. The only requirement is that the coloring of the ribbon provides a blending contrast between the natural coloring of the fringed mat and the cured gourds. Choose durable materials, and you will have a wreath that lasts for years.

Testing the Rope

Before making the wreath, cut one 10½-inch section of rope and make a fringe knot to one loop on the mat. See the following method for fringing the mat. Should you have a tightly twisted rope that resists forming a fringe knot, follow the directions in Method I for fringing the mat. Photographs in this series show the wreath being made using Method I, but if the 10½-inch strand of rope easily forms a fringe knot, employ the simple steps under Method II.

Here are the many materials you may use to make an Ornamental gourd wreath: 16-inch-round woven mat with looped edge (craft or florist's shop), ⅜-inch-wide Manila rope, 24–26-gauge florist's wire (preferable a dark color), 7 yards of 2-inch decorative ribbon, masking tape, small pinecones or sweet gum balls, a Crown of Thorns gourd, small assorted Ornamental gourds such as Apple, Pear, and Egg. Optional materials for the motif are six ears of strawberry corn and two small ears of Ornamental corn. Other materials include paste wax for wood, electric drill with thin bit, wire cutters, utility knife (jigsaw or sharp kitchen knife), and scissors.

Fringing the mat

Method I

With a utility knife, jigsaw, or sharp kitchen knife, cut twenty-eight 10½-inch strands of Manila rope for a 16-inch mat. Untwist the three strands in each section of rope; soak them in warm water until they are soft and pliable. Then fringe two strands of rope over each extending loop on the edge of the mat.

Method II

With a utility knife, jigsaw, or sharp kitchen knife, cut thirty-six 10½-inch strands of rope, one for each loop on the edge of the mat. Fringe-knot each 3-ply strand directly onto each loop extending from the mat.

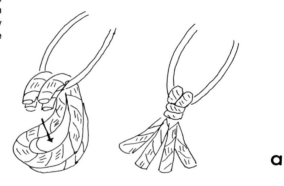

a

To make a fringe knot, fold *a* tne double strand (Method I) or *b* the 3-ply strand (Method II) of rope in half. Push the folded end of rope down through the loop on the mat. Bend the fold beneath to meet the ends of rope. Open the fold to make a loop and insert the ends of rope through the hole. Tighten the fringe by pushing the knot back with one hand while pulling the ends of rope with the other. Be careful not to pull the free end of the extending loop from the mat.

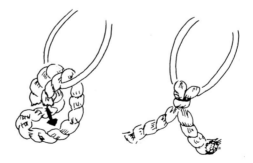

b

Method I

After all the loops around the mat are fringed, cut twelve 11½-inch strands of rope. Untwist the three strands of each section of rope; soak the single strands in warm water until they soften. Knot only one 11½-inch strand in opening x between the adjacent loops on the mat.

Method II

Cut 36 strands of rope 11½ inches long. Fringe-knot opening x between each loop on the mat with a strand of 3-ply rope.

Straightening the fringe. Unravel, then take apart the components of each rope attached to the mat. When finished, sponge the circle of fringe with warm water. Let the water soak through the fibers. Then gently comb the Manila fibers until they are straight and smooth. Let the fringe dry overnight. Finish the fringe by trimming uneven and loose ends with a scissors.

Hanging device. Turn the mat to the back side. Fix the hanging device through the solid round of weaving on the upper portion of the mat. To form the hanging device, cover a 12-inch section of double wire with masking tape. Bend the covered wire in half. Insert the two ends of wire down, then up through the woven part of the mat. Then twist the free ends up over the base of the folded loop. Remember the placement of the hanging device later when you wire the motif to the right side of the mat.

Attaching the loops of ribbons. Prewire a series of loops before attaching them to the mat. To form a loop, use 5 to 6 inches of ribbon. Tie it tightly at the bottom with a 9-inch strand of wire. Allowing a 3-inch length of ribbon between each loop, continue forming the loops in the same manner with a separate wire for each one. The circle of looped ribbon should cover the knots of fringe only three-quarters of the way around the mat, leaving one-quarter free for the motif. When you have made enough loops for the three-quarter circle, wire each loop to the open strands on the mat. Just use the wires tied to each loop.

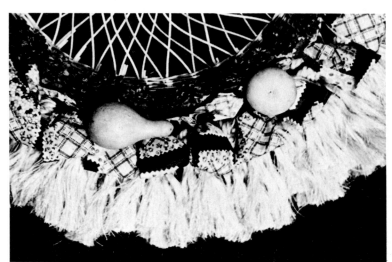

Wiring cones to the mat. First wire the cones separately before tying them to the mat. Cut a 10-inch length of wire and wind it 1½ times tightly through the scales at the base of the cone. When finished, the ends of wire should be opposite each other. After the cones are wired properly, attach them side by side to the next area of tight weaving on the mat. The cones are placed directly beneath the circle of ribbon, again leaving one-quarter of the mat free for the motif.

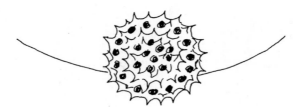

Variation: A circle of sweet gum balls may be substituted for the row of small pinecones. Drill a hole straight through a one third section of each prickly ball; insert a 10-inch strand of wire through the opening. Wire the balls to the mat beneath the circle of ribbon.

Prepare the small Ornamental gourds by soaking them in hot water until their outer skins have softened. Then scrape the papery skin and mold from each gourd carefully with a knife and steel wool pad. After the gourds are dry, polish them with paste wax. Then drill two holes into each gourd about 1 inch apart. Bend the tip of a 14-inch section of wire and insert it through the holes in the gourd.

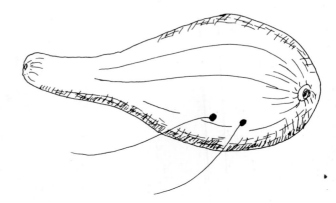

Freely place the gourds at equal intervals over the circle of looped ribbon. When you are satisfied with their appearance, wire each gourd over the ribbon, twisting the ends of wire together under the mat.

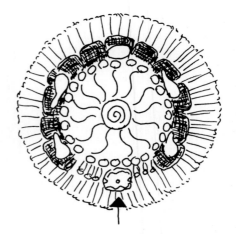

Combining the motif. Wire the Crown of Thorns gourd first to the middle of the empty space reserved for the motif.

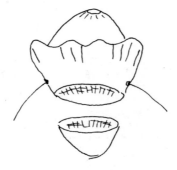

If the gourd is too tall, cut off the base with a sharp paring knife. Drill holes through the opposite sides, close to the bottom opening of the gourd. Insert a long piece of wire through the two holes, and wire the gourd to the mat.

Combine two bunches of corn, one for each side of the motif. Wire three ears of strawberry corn over an extending ear of small Ornamental corn. If you are using other plant materials, tie them in bunches whenever possible; then attach them to the mat. Masking tape will also hold materials together, when necessary.

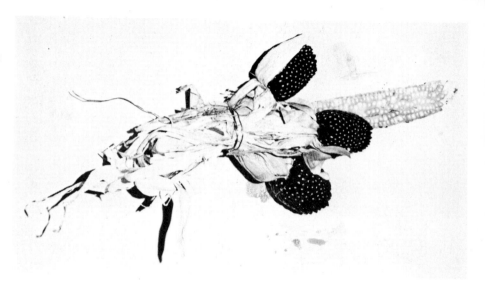

Hide the wire mechanics and masking tape with loops of prewired ribbon. Place these gatherings of ribbon on both sides of the Crown of Thorns, covering the wired husks—and the wreath is complete. As a final finishing touch, push all free ends of wire through the weaving of the mat.

A variety of Lagenaria and Ornamental gourds.

An interesting variety of cured Lagenaria. The outer skin and crust have not yet been cleaned from their surfaces.

John Kraft's home in Landskrona, Sweden, is effectively landscaped with a bed of bright flowers below and vines with hanging pale green Lagenaria above. Courtesy, John Kraft

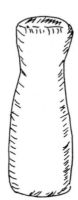
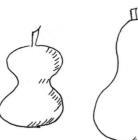

Knob Kerrie, Swan, Zucca, Dumbbell, African Kettle.

Cured Lagenarias. *Back row:* Round warty, Watermelon, Cannonball, small Kettle. *Front:* Fish or Maranka.

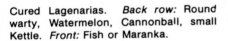

Lagenaria: The Hardshelled Gourd

The Lagenarias are called Hardshelled gourds because their large fruits dry to a thin, solid waterproof shell. The varied sizes and shapes of Lagenarias suggest their usefulness as containers, utensils, and other items. With reasonable care, they should last indefinitely.

Hardshelled gourds are green to yellow while maturing on the vine. They become off-white or beige to brown after harvesting or curing on lifeless vines. While Lagenarias are still fresh, they are over 90 percent water. The larger ones have a high moisture content and become quite heavy. Immense gourds weighing over a hundred pounds surprisingly dehydrate to only a couple of pounds when cured.

Gourds that are cured have a thin, hard exterior with a thicker, soft white layer beneath. Their hard, woody shells, suitable for cutting and decorating, are treated in the same manner as wood.

Like Ornamentals, Lagenarias are named according to their shapes. Though there are many more types of gourds and mixes, the following chart is a comprehensive list of the most common Hardshelled gourds:

Bottle gourd, or Chinese Water Jug. The general description of a Bottle gourd is that it is restricted in the center. Its lower body is enlarged or globular. When the Bottle gourd has upper and lower chambers approximately the same size, it is called a Dumbbell or Ipi Nui (Hawaiian Drum gourd). Four types of Bottle gourds, differing in shape, originated in each of the following places: Mexico, Africa, Costa Rica, and Hawaii.

Club gourds are long and narrow and generally larger at one end than the other. They are straight when grown off the ground, but curved when they mature on the earth. Three types of Club gourds are:

Cave Man's Club—bat-shaped gourd
Hercules Club—extra long, cylindrical gourd
Knob Kerrie—long slender club with handle at one end.

45

Cured Bottle, Penguin, and Baseball Bat. The outer skin and crust have not yet been cleaned from their surfaces.

The painted black and white penguin is made from a Penguin gourd.

Dolphin, Moranka, or *Fish* is a dolphin-shaped gourd with ridges at the broad end and a straight or curved narrow handle.

Penguins, Powder Horns, are curved gourds with gradual enlargement at one end. They are often painted with black and white enamel to resemble a penguin.

Snakes are slender curved gourds that are usually grown on the ground. They are often manipulated by hand to look more like a winding snake. Green snakes often grow to ten feet in length. Snakes, or Serpents, are generally five feet.

Swan gourds have ball-shaped bases with slender, winding necks.
Tobacco Box, Canteen Gourd, Jewel Box, Sugar Bowls are round gourds that are flat on the bottom and on the top. They range from small to very large.

Bushel Basket, Kettle, Calabash, are huge pumpkin-shaped gourds, which when mature can weigh over a hundred pounds. They have been used throughout history as containers or baskets.

Zucca. Tall curved drum-shaped gourd.
Trough, Watermelon, are broad cylindrical gourds rounded at both ends.

Ball gourds are spherical in shape:
    Baseballs or   Small round
    Cannonballs   gourds
    Basketball—larger spherical gourds.

Siphon, Dipper, or *Retort* has a long narrow neck with a ball at one end. When the gourd is grown on the ground, its handle is curved. If it is grown from a trellis, the handle is straight.

Large and small cured Tobacco Box, Canteen, or Jewelry Box. The small ones are often called Sugar Bowls.

The small Bottle gourd, decorated with a burnt design, is one of the smallest Lagenarias. Larue Stith

Growing long-handled Dipper gourds. Courtesy, J. S. Story

The short-handled Dipper has an opening cut into the ball end so that the gourd may be used as a dipper or ladle. The long-handled Dipper with a winding handle is grown on the ground. The straight handle of the Dipper gourd is obtained by growing the gourd from a trellis.

Fresh green Bushel Basket, Kettle, Bowl, or Calabash gourds.

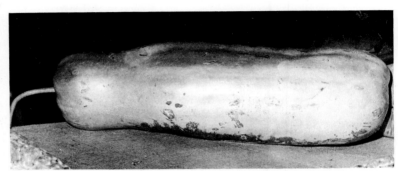

Zucca gourd.

Pale green Costa Rican Bottle gourds.

Freshly harvested plain and marbled Snake gourds.

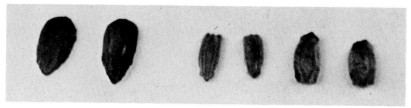

Gourd seeds. The first two are large almond-shaped seeds from a Kettle gourd. The remaining seeds are curved and patterned seeds found in most types of Lagenarias. They vary in size and color.

Planting Lagenaria Seeds

Seeds are not usually available at nurseries or supermarkets. However, you may purchase gourd seeds from seed companies listed in the Sources of Supply. Another way to obtain seed is to contact experienced gourd growers. Some are listed in the American Gourd Society's publication, *The Gourd.*

The Lagenarias need a longer growing season to mature than Ornamentals. In southern states or in the tropics the seeds may be planted outdoors at the start of the growing season. There the gourds will completely ripen on the vine. In zone 4,* where the growing season lasts 140 days, seeds are sown indoors in cartons or flats, then the small vines are planted outside after the last frost. Regions with short growing seasons, which include the northern United States and Canada, may start their plants in greenhouses. With proper instruction, Hardshelled gourds can be grown successfully in temperate climates.

Planting in Cooler Climates

In areas having a 140-day growing season, sow the seed indoors about three to four weeks before the last frost. Many gourd growers have difficulty getting their gourds to germinate in a reasonable amount of time—from eight to ten days. Since it is important that gourds have as long a growing season as possible, you can hasten germination by placing seeds between layers of wet flannel or terry towel. Then put the covered seeds in a warm place for a day and a half and keep the fabric moist. Plant the seeds that sprout one-half inch below the soil's surface in a container or flat with plenty of good potting soil.

Testing the seed can be very important in northern states. If you have bad seed, it is often too late to replant and get mature gourds in the fall. So five months before planting time, place six seeds of each type in a wet towel until they sprout. Keep the covered seeds in a warm place and the towel moist. Eighty percent germination is necessary for a successful planting.

One way to plant gourds is in large half-gallon cartons or huge peat pots with plastic bags over them to retain their moisture. The covered cartons are kept in a warm place until plants appear above the soil. The seeds may take from ten days to a month, sometimes more, to germinate. After the plants can be seen well above the surface, remove the plastic

* Zones of hardiness for woody plants can be found in *Taylor's Encyclopedia of Gardening* and *Wyman's Gardening Encyclopedia.*

bags and place the containers in a sunny window. From now on, the plants require water when the soil becomes dry.

After the last frost has passed, two or three plants may be transplanted outside in mounds of soil spaced ten feet apart. For vigorous growth and greater production, place a shovelful of well-rotted manure beneath the planting surface of each mound. The seeds that sprout in the original top soil form roots which will receive nutrients from the rotted manure beneath. Some gourd growers work nitrogen fertilizer around each mound of soil to give the vines a good start, but a high nitrogen fertilizer should not be added later because it encourages vines rather than gourds to grow.

The young plants can be covered with paper, glass, or plastic at night if there is an unexpected danger of frost. Gourd vines resent being transplanted and will not grow for the first few weeks or so. As soon as the vines start to grow, they will make remarkable progress.

Planting in Warmer Climates

The best location for growing Lagenaria plants is in rich, well-drained mounds of soil spaced ten feet apart under full sunlight. A shovelful of well-rotted manure can be placed directly under the planting surface of each mound. The seeds that sprout in the original top soil form roots that will receive nutrients from the rotted manure beneath. Another way to enrich the soil is by working nitrogen fertilizer around the edge of each mound where the fertilizer will not touch the seeds. Nitrogen fertilizer should not be added later, since it encourages vines rather than gourds to grow.

Sow about eight seeds in each hill to allow for poor germination and other hazards. Cover the seeds with one-half to one inch of soil according to the size of the seed. A good depth is two times the length of the seed. After the seeds sprout, allow them to grow into small plants. Then thin down each hill to two or three of the strongest plants, as long as they are well separated.

Planting Tips

Lagenarias do not cross-pollinate with Ornamental gourds, so they may be planted nearby. However, different varieties of Lagenarias do cross. If you wish to keep a pure stock, each type should be planted in a different area of land with plenty of space between.

When a variety of Hardshelled gourds are planted in the same spot, you can control the strains early in the season by hand pollination. It is also a relief to know that gourds do not interpollinate with other members of the Cucurbitaceae family—pumpkins, squash, cucumbers, or melons.

Planting gourd seeds. Pour water into a large container that is filled with a good potting soil.

After watering the soil thoroughly, cover each seed with ½ inch of soil and press down.

Insert the planted cartons or pots into plastic bags and allow them to germinate in a warm place. Germination generally occurs within two to five weeks.

When the plant appears above the surface, set the carton in a warm, sunny window. Water the plant as needed, until the vine can be transplanted outside.

The Growing Lagenaria

Gourd vines with their broad leaves and long extending tendrils develop so quickly you can almost see them grow. Because their tendrils cling and wind onto nearby objects, they can be trained to grow off the ground on trellises, arbors, fences, on wire or rope between two poles, over arched chicken wire, up stone walls and dead trees. Smaller Lagenaria, when grown off the ground, will have a more uniform color and less blemishes than those grown on the ground. Some large strains become so heavy that they must mature on the ground. Giant gourds, such as the Zucca, African Bushel Basket, and Wine Kettle can get so heavy that the vines on a trellis cannot support them. Plastic sheets or straw placed under the gourds help prevent discoloration and possible rotting.

Most gourd cultivators produce more gourds from each plant when the central vine is cut off at eight to ten feet. This action will stimulate the growth of new extending branches with more female blossoms to pollinate. A few gourd growers pinch off the main vine as soon as it reaches fifteen inches, so that the plant will produce more lateral and sublaterals. They believe that the best results are achieved by allowing only four to five gourds to mature on one vine.

To achieve the long, straight handle on the Dipper gourds, the gourds are grown from a trellis. A straw mulch is laid under the trellis to preserve the moisture and to keep down weeds. Courtesy, J. S. Story

A broad green leaf extending from a gourd vine.

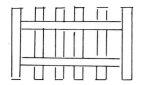 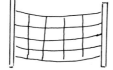 

Gourd plants may be raised off the ground over fences or arched wire meshes.

To help prevent discoloration and infestation, a sheet of plastic is placed under the gourd that grows on the ground.

Uncut gourd vines, particularly large species, can grow as high as four stories.

Pungent white blossoms of the Lagenaria plant open during the evenings, on gray cloud-covered days and sometimes during the early morning hours for pollination.

Diseases

Gourd plants are often affected by the same insects and diseases as other Cucurbitaceae; particularly cucumber beetles, aphids, squash bugs, mildew, wilt, and borers. Most are controlled early with dust or spray; Sevin or another similar product will give good results. Spray under the leaves as well as on top. Treat the plants after a rain until they become two to three feet in length. Be careful not to dust young gourds since chemicals can burn their skin.

Borers occasionally get inside the vine near the root and cause the plant to die. A hole that oozes moisture will show the presence of a borer. Sometimes it is possible to slit the vine carefully, cut out the borer, and cover the vine with wet dirt. An insecticide squirted with a medicine dropper may kill the worm and save the vine. As a precaution, pile some soil over one or two joints of the vine near the root. New roots will grow there and may save the life of the vine.

Rotating the gourds from one planting area to another each year will help eliminate much of the insect problem.

Female and male blossoms.

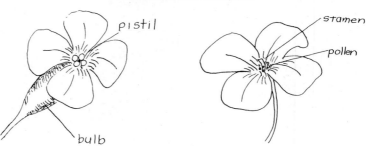

Pollinating Female Flowers

White musky-smelling male flowers are the first to appear on the main vine. A series of female flowers later develop as offshoots from the main vine. The female blossoms open during the evening hours for pollination, sometimes on dark, dreary days and early mornings.

If the bees are not pollinating the female flowers early in the season, you will find it an easy and enjoyable pastime to pollinate them yourself during the evening. By hand pollination you may control and retain a pure stock when assorted gourds are planted close by.

After pollination, the petals dry and the shape of the gourd in miniature can be viewed immediately. At that time the gourd is only a couple of inches long.

A growing Hercules Club.

To pollinate the female flower, first capture the pollen surrounding the stamen of the male flower with a small artist's brush. Then brush the pollen over the four-pronged pistil of the female blossom. After the growing season is well under way, the flowering gourd patch usually attracts a swarm of bees that willingly take over the task of pollination.

After the female flower is pollinated and the petals wilt, the shape of the growing gourd may be determined by viewing the bulbous form beneath the fallen petals. Throughout the growing season, new gourds will appear as the plant continues to produce vegetation and flowering blossoms.

A knot can be tied with a long handle of a Dipper gourd after several days of hot, dry weather. Usually, a knot is formed the first day, then tightened the next. Sometimes a weight is placed at both ends to hold the knot in place. Courtesy, J. S. Story

Curved handles of Dipper gourds are the results of growing the gourds on the ground. Slings are used to obtain a desired shape. Long-handled Dippers with interesting contorted handles are excellent for use in abstract arrangements. Courtesy, J. S. Story

Controlling the Size and Shape of the Growing Gourd

If you desire larger gourds, allow only a few gourds to mature on the vine. Cut off the extending branches with blossoming female flowers after a couple of female blossoms have been successfully pollinated.

The shape of the gourd can be altered in many ways as the gourd grows. One way to control the shape of the gourd has already been discussed with the Dipper gourd at the beginning of this chapter. When a gourd is allowed to hang by its neck while it is growing, the neck will become very long and straight. Gourds growing on the ground naturally curve more and are bulkier.

A gentle working with the fingers daily during the hottest part of the day will help curve the gourd to the desired form. The process can be aided, for example, with Dipper gourds where long handled curves are tied with a strip of fabric. Tieing areas of the gourd with strips of cloth helps control the shape in another way. Different chambers can be made by constricting the gourd horizontally or vertically with strips of fabric or rope as the gourd grows.

A knot can be tied with the long handle of a Dipper when the weather is hot and dry. The first day the handle is tied into a knot; the second day the knot is tightened and possibly weighted at both ends.

Cured and painted Snake. The Snake gourd was shaped while it was growing. Courtesy, Museum of Marvin Johnson

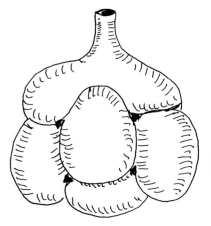

The resulting effect occurs when the Lagenaria is wound with rope while it is growing.

A gourd may be altered by pressure. The gourd will have a level bottom if placed on a flat stone or a board while it is growing. Gourds grown in containers will take the shape of the container. A gourd may be grown in a bottle, which can be broken when the gourd fills the bottle. The method works particularly well when the summer is not too humid.

In addition, if a gourd is grown in a box, it will take the shape of the box. Once the gourd is shaped by the box, it will continue to take the form of the box as it grows. Years ago Chinese Cricket gourds were grown in ancient clay molds, often with incised decoration on the inside. Not only would the gourd take the shape of the mold, but the incised design of the clay mold made a beautiful relief. The shapely gourd can be viewed at the museum of Marvin Johnson in Fuquay Varina, North Carolina, and Cricket molds are part of the collection at Salem's Peabody Museum.

Another method of shaping a gourd from a mold can be found in the book *Gourds, Decorative and Edible for Garden, Craftwork and Table*, by John Organ. The book describes how to make a plaster mold for a growing gourd.

Decorating the gourd may be started while it is still green. An incised design accomplished on a gourd while it is green will remain during the life of the gourd. In Africa, a design is carved on the wall of a green gourd, after the gourd is colored with a natural dye. When the Lagenaria becomes dry, the smooth surface of the gourd is lighter and the incised design is darker in color. The dye only slightly penetrates the smooth surface of the gourd, while the coloring easily is absorbed by the white layer beneath.

The violin gourd body was grown in a mold. Courtesy, Museum of Marvin Johnson

Harvesting Hardshelled Gourds

Since Lagenarias in southern states have lengthy growing seasons, the gourds will be yellow to brown when they are ready to harvest. The gourds may be picked at that time, or they may be allowed to dry in the field.

Lagenarias in northern states are often picked while they are still green. In cooler areas gourds should remain in the garden as long as there is any life in the vine. Some gourd growers believe that gourds remaining in the garden throughout the winter become improved for craft purposes.

One exception: Any gourd clinging high over a stone wall or similar vertical construction should be harvested while the vines are still alive and green. Otherwise the gourds may fall from great heights and become damaged after the frost, when the vine dies and the tendrils no longer have their holding powers.

To harvest a gourd, cut it from the vine with clippers, a sharp knife, or scissors, leaving at least a two-inch stem on the fruit.

Gourds and vines not harvested by the following growing season should be completely removed so that insects and disease will not carry over into the next year's crop.

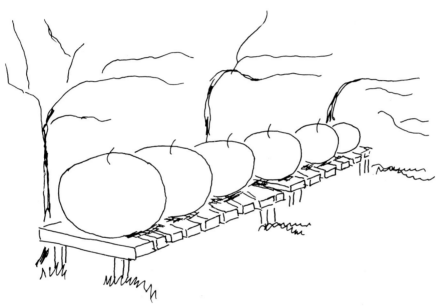

Marvin Johnson, expert gourd culturist, cures his Lagenaria Kettles and other large gourds on racks in the field during the winter.

Curing Gourds

Most smaller Hardshelled gourds take from three to six months to dry. Some Lagenarias grow so large that the curing time takes more than a year. As the gourds dry, they turn from pale green or gold to beige or brown.

To cure gourds, place them on a rack—indoors or out—where air can circulate around them. Marvin Johnson cures many large Basket gourds on racks in the fields through the mild North Carolina winter.

If you have harvested only a few gourds, place them on layers of absorbent newspapers. Turn the gourds at intervals to expose all sides to the air. Some gourds may be hung in decorative mesh coverings, such as onion, potato, or turkey sacks.

Mr. Johnson dries some of his gourds in tobacco barns at the constant temperature of 95 to 100 degrees. They dry in weeks to a different consistency. Musical instruments made with these gourds have a different tone.

As the gourds dry, their surface develops characteristic dark spots, which adds to their beauty when their crust is removed. While the gourds are curing, they may benefit from an occasional wiping with Lysol disinfectant, diluted with water.

Lagenarias are dry when they turn off-white, natural beige, or brown. This change in color is accompanied by a hardening of the shell. Gourds are dry when they are light in weight and their seeds rattle.

Other Methods of Curing and Preparing Gourds

AFRICAN METHODS

Nigerian
Mature gourds are harvested, then soaked in water until the contents rot. After the gourds are opened and the pulp is removed, they are left to dry in the sun.

Ghanan
After a ripe gourd is picked, an opening is cut in the top. Then water is poured inside to facilitate the rotting of the pulp. After the material is cleaned from the inside of the gourd, it is left to dry in the hot sun.

SOUTH SEA ISLANDS AND NEW ZEALAND

When the gourds are picked, they are dried near a fire, by the sun, or else they are buried in sandy or gravelly soil. After the gourds are cleaned with gravel, they are hung to harden near a fire.

The old Maori Indian method of curing gourds was to bury them in warm, dry sand until all the moisture drained into the sand—about four to five months. Sand was renewed at intervals. Other gourds were opened as soon as they were picked, after which all the pulp was carefully scraped out.

HAWAII

Gourds used as containers were classed as "sweet" or "bitter." "Bitter" gourds were cleaned out completely and allowed to dry. After the gourd was cured, the remaining material was scraped with pumice or coral. Bitter gourds were filled with freshwater or seawater until the bitterness vanished.

Hawaiians extracted the pulp through a narrow opening of the gourd water bottle by first pouring water into the gourd to hasten the decaying process. Next, sand or stones were deposited in the gourd and bounced around inside. After freeing the pulp from the inner wall in this manner, the contents (seed and pulp) were eliminated.

The painted vase has openings in the gourd wall as part of the design. Captain Alfred Chenney. Courtesy, Museum of Marvin Johnson

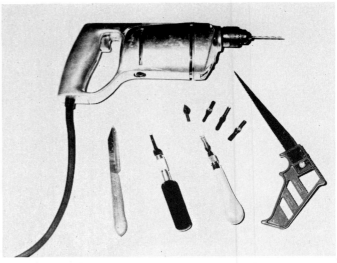

Tools used for cutting and sawing Hardshelled gourds are an electric drill with bit, pointed paring knife, hand wood cutting tools and gouges (or linoleum block cutting tools), and a keyhole saw.

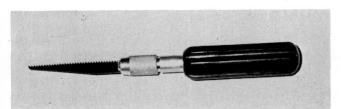

The X-acto handle with a toothed cutting blade is ideal for sawing almost any type of gourd, whether the wall is thick or thin, soft or hard.

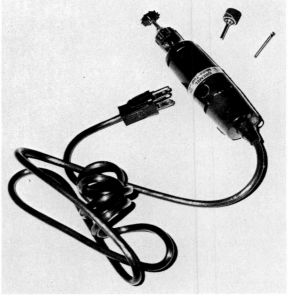

The electric Dremel Moto tool may be used for gourd crafting with the following accessories: round saw blade for cutting openings in large gourds, sanding cylinder for smoothing rims, and ball tip for carving. Protect your eyes from sawdust with goggles and your nose and mouth with a scarf.

The fine engraver for the Dremel Moto tool is used in the next chapter to engrave the Leave-a-Note Box.

Tools and Methods

This chapter is devoted entirely to such fundamentals as cutting, joining, sculpturing, waterproofing, leveling, hinging, attaching hardware, and weighting. These basic mechanics will provide knowledge for creating vases, bowls, planters, baskets, sculptures, musical instruments, jewelry, and more from gourds. Application of crafting tools and techniques are illustrated in chapters 6, 7, and 8. Throughout the book gourds are treated in the same manner as wood, but smaller scale tools are needed so that the gourds will not be damaged in the process.

Cutting and Sawing Cured Gourds

Gourds may be cut horizontally, vertically, or any other way your imagination says to proceed to produce the type of container desired. Because each gourd is different, you will need to use your own aesthetic judgment as to where the cutting line should be.

Many different types of tools may be used to cut openings into the gourd wall, each having its own advantages and disadvantages. Hand tools for cutting or sawing are a pocket or paring knife, X-acto handle with saw blade, keyhole saw, or the electrical Dremel Moto tool with the round sawing disk.

The opening in a soft or medium-walled gourd can usually be cut with a pointed paring or pocket knife. If the wall is hard and solid, a hole is drilled into the gourd large enough to insert a fine saw blade. The advantage of starting the cut with a knife is that the cut is smooth and straight; a hole drilled with a bit will produce a little round nick—which could be bothersome.

Once you experiment with the pocket or paring knife, you will be able to assess the density of the gourd and select the best cutting tool for

After marking the gourd for the placement of holes with a pencil, start each opening with an awl, pointed tip of a knife, or an ice pick.

Place the bit into the indentation; then drill the hole through the gourd wall.

the purpose. A paring or pocket knife can easily be used for soft gourds; tools with saw blades are better for hard-walled gourds.

While cutting or sawing, you may find one side of the gourd thicker and harder than the other. Less pressure is applied when cutting the thinner side so that the wall will not crack. If the gourd should crack while cutting, you may find the resulting form even better than the original. The scalloped bowl in chapter 6 with the fruit inside was the result of a comedy of errors. Though the bowl did not measure up to the preconceived idea, it turned out unusually delightful.

Some craftspeople make an opening for a gourd container by sawing the gourd over a stationary clamped saw, turning the gourd as it is cut. Their goal is to achieve an even rim for a bowl, platter, or vase.

Drilling Holes in the Gourd Wall

Use an awl only to start a hole. After making an indentation with a pointed tool or awl, a small hole in the gourd may be made with an ice pick, hand or electric drill, or a Dremel-Moto tool with a pointed tip. Avoid using an awl to make a complete opening, since its broad conical point may crack the gourd wall.

Joining Gourds and Their Parts

GLUING

Clear glues—such as Duco cement, Sobo Crafts glue, epoxy glue for woods—are good for cementing gourd handles, extensions, and extremities onto gourd bodies. Other glues that work well on wood may also be used for gourds. While the cement dries, the parts may be held together with masking tape.

SEWING

Access to the inside cavities of the gourds is needed when gourds are joined by the sewing method. Drill a succession of holes into the parts to be joined, then sew them together with strong thread, cord, or yarn.

COIL WEAVING

Coil weaving is another method for attaching gourds together and provides a cylindrical extension between the gourds. Each gourd needs an opening large enough for a hand to work through. A series of holes is drilled around the opening of each gourd. After the weaving is completed on one gourd, the last row of weaving is sewn onto the other gourd. Coil weaving was used as a means of attaching gourds together in the hanging sculpture in chapter 7.

NAILS AND SCULPTAMOLD (AMACO) ®

Sculptamold is a powder which when mixed with water can be used to smoothly join gourds and their parts. This white powder can be purchased in a plastic bag at arts and crafts stores.

To join gourds and their parts, first fasten the joint together with small nails. Then cover the joint with a soft mixture of Sculptamold: four parts Sculptamold and three parts water. After the connection is dry in approximately a half hour, the hardened Sculptamold can be sanded, then coated with any paint that matches the color of the gourds.

The nail-Sculptamold combination is good for making abstract sculptures, animals, and people. Minnie Black, a gourd artist whose animals and people are pictured in this book, devised this technique.

GLUE-SOAKED COTTON AND PLASTIC WOOD

Plastic wood is available at hardware stores in varied shades of brown. Choose the shade that will most closely match the coloring of the gourds involved. Though plastic wood will not usually hold gourds and their parts together alone, it can be used to cover the glued cotton and will blend with the coloring of the gourd.

First file the joints before applying the glue-soaked cotton. Soak a long wad of cotton with glue and place it over the joint. Continue applying the cotton in this manner until the joint is completely covered. If necessary, use masking tape to hold the parts together while applying the cotton and until the cotton dries.

When the joint is dry, apply plastic wood over the connection to give it a natural finish. If the coloring of the plastic wood does not quite blend with the gourd, it may be painted the desired color with artists' acrylic paints.

HINGING

Small hinges, purchased at hardware or craft stores, may be used to attach a pre-sawed door to the gourd wall. Instead of using the small nails in the package, purchase tiny nuts and bolts that will fit into holes of the hinges. The nuts act as reinforcement for the gourd wall. When the gourd wall is particularly thin, reinforce it with a piece of cardboard glued to the inside of the gourd. Or else use a washer under the nut when the bolt is screwed into the gourd wall.

If the bolts are slightly broader in diameter than the openings in the hinges, enlarge the holes with an electric drill using a bit slightly larger than the width of the holes.

The central pivots of both hinges must lie vertically or horizontally in a straight line between the gourd wall and the door. After making indentations through the openings of the hinge with an awl or ice pick, make holes for the bolts through the gourd wall and door with the drill. It

The hinge is held in place by nuts and bolts. The nuts on the inside wall of the gourd act as reinforcement.

The hinge and closing device are used on the elegantly decorated Peruvian box. Courtesy, Museo Nacional de la Cultura Peruana. Photographed by Seno Wilfredo Loaza

The small hinge is attached to the door and the corresponding gourd wall.

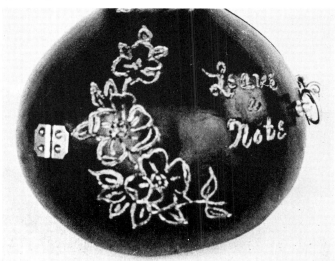

is better to drill holes for the hinges before the door is cut out to lessen breakage, though it is not absolutely necessary. See the directions for the Leave-a-Note Box.

HARDWARE FOR OPENING HINGED DOORS

A wide variety of different handles, from decorative hanging screws to drawer handles, can be purchased at hardware stores for opening a hinged door. Shorter bolts must be purchased separately to attach drawer handles to gourds, for the gourd wall is much thinner than the wood from which furniture is made. Larger round washers help hold the hardware in place as well as providing reinforcement for the gourd wall.

HARDWARE FOR CLOSING HINGED DOORS

Clasps, hasps, or swivel locks may be purchased at crafts or leather stores. Hooks and eyes, also used to close hinged doors, may be purchased at selected hardware stores.

WEIGHTING

For gourd lamp bases or sculptures, the gourds should be weighted at the bottom so that they will not tip over. One method is to mix plaster of Paris with water until it forms a thick cream. Then pour the plaster into the bottom of the gourd. Put the remaining plaster in newspaper and throw it into the waste can.

Another procedure is to mix four parts Sculptamold with three parts water, then add small stones and fishing weights to the mix. Push the components into the gourd while the Sculptamold is still soft.

Another method of weighting gourds is to apply a heavy base to the bottom of the gourd, such as a heavy round of hardwood or weighted lamp base. Weights for lamp bases may be purchased separately at hardware stores.

LEVELING

When it is necessary to level the base of the gourd so that it does not tilt, use one of the following methods:
1. File small areas beneath the gourd where the feet are to be placed. Then apply wads of plastic wood over the roughened areas for "feet." Place the feet apart at the correct distance and adjust them to the right height to ensure balance. Feet may also be made from cork disks or small pieces of wood.
2. Saw or cut a level opening in the bottom of the gourd so that it stands erect—or in another desirable position. Glue or nail the proper size plywood round to the bottom of the gourd.

OTHER BASES FOR GOURD PROJECTS

Besides making "feet" or applying hardwood or lamp bases, gourd projects can be fitted with other types of interesting bases:
1. Nonskid caster cups, usually used under legs of furniture to protect the floor, can be purchased at hardware stores. They are generally available in two colors, pale beige or dark brown. After the gourd is prebalanced over the cup, the caster cup is glued to the base of the gourd with Duco or epoxy cement for wood.
2. After a hole is drilled beneath the gourd, it may be fitted over or on top of a pedestal. To make a pedestal, a hole—the diameter of the dowel—is drilled in the center of a wooden block. Next the dowel is glued and fitted into the opening.
3. A handmade or purchased basket that partially encases the gourd will provide a base to hold the gourd erect.
4. The most natural base for a gourd project is to use a shapely slice of another gourd and glue it to the bottom.

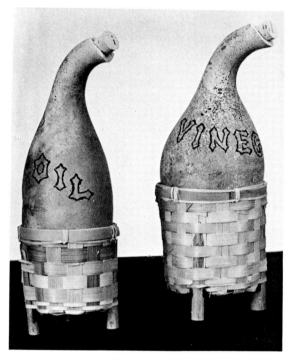

Vinegar and oil set. Two smooth Penguin gourds are fitted upright into standing baskets. A narrow opening on the top of each gourd is cut on a slant for pouring. The lettering *vinegar and oil* is done with a wood burner. Carolyn Mordecai

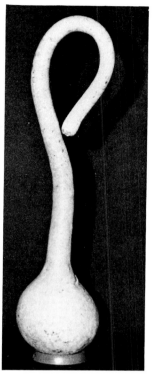

A caster cup, glued to the base of the Dipper, holds the gourd erect.

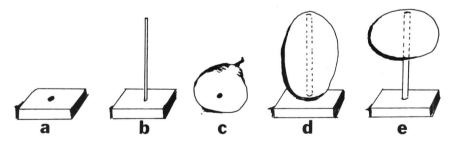

To make a pedestal: *a.* First drill a hole the diameter of the dowel in the middle of a wooden block. *b.* Insert a dowel into the hole with a little glue. *c.* Cut or drill the hole—again the diameter of the dowel—into the bottom of the gourd. *d.* Fit the gourd over the dowel so that it rests on top of the wooden base. *e.* Or else, fit the gourd over the top of the dowel so that the pedestal base can be seen.

The carved and burnt animal, made from a Tobacco Box gourd, rests over a hidden pedestal. Carnegie Institute, Museum Shops and Raquel's Collection

The carved and burnt bird from Peru sits on an open pedestal. Courtesy, Carnegie Institute, Museum Shops and Raquel's Collection

The geometrically designed burnt vase rests on a natural pedestal cut from another gourd. Larue Stith

The freely decorated vase has a gourd opening and base covered with gourd seed. John Kraft

Finishing the Inner Wall of the Gourd Container

The inside of the gourd is usually smoothed patiently with heavy to fine sandpaper. Sometimes stones, pumice, or coral is used to take extra material from the inside of the gourd.

Waterproofing the Interior

The inside of gourd vessels usually do not require any other finish but a good sanding. The need for waterproofing depends on whether the inner wall is subjected to constant moisture; for example, a planter.

To protect a planter from the soil's moisture, pour paraffin inside; then roll the wax until the cavity is completely covered. Pour the remaining hot wax in the can and wipe the inside of the pan with a paper towel while it is still hot. Do not be tempted to pour hot wax down the drain, for it will clog the pipes. A sheet of aluminum foil fitted inside the planter will also prevent moisture from soaking in the gourd wall.

Many paints for woods can be used effectively to coat the inside of the gourd as long as the wall is well sanded.

The Bottle gourd in a three-legged stand is a reminder of the Maori bird preserver of New Zealand. The shapely gourd is raised above the surface on a sling extending down from three tent pegs. Two rounds of metal stripping keep the tent pegs in place.

To construct a Maori-style stand, you will need the following materials: *1.* Leather or vinyl material. *2.* Metal strips or weather stripping with *3.* Nails. (A heavy duty staple gun with staples can be used to attach the stripping to the tent pegs instead of nails.) *4.* Three or four tent pegs. *5.* Heavy cord, leather strips, or jute. *6.* A shapely gourd. Tent pegs are sold where camping equipment is for sale.

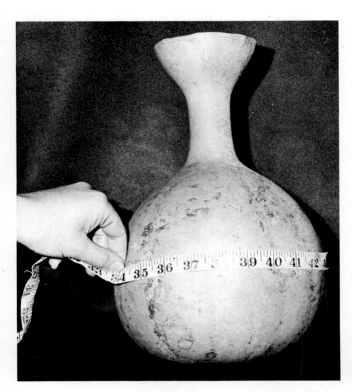

a. Measure the diameter of the gourd at its broadest width.

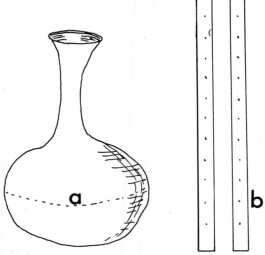

b. Cut two metal strips a few inches larger than the width of the gourd. If you are using copper stripping, be sure that the holes are in the same place in both strips. The holes can be used as measuring guides for the placement of the tent pegs.

72

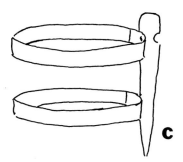

c

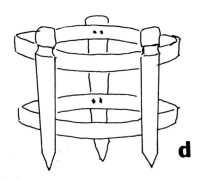

d

c. Overlap the ends of each copper strip; staple or nail the ends of both strips to the first tent peg. Be sure that the crevice at the top of the tent peg faces the outside. Place the two strips so that they are parallel with a space between them. Remember that the tent pegs should be on the outside and the rounds of stripping on the inside of the construction.

d. Staple or nail the stripping to the other pegs, spacing them equally around each circle of the stripping. Use the holes in the copper strips as a measuring guide. Attach the strips to the tent pegs in the same places on the pegs as the first tent peg. Always be sure that the crevices at the top of the tent pegs face the outside.

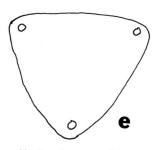

e

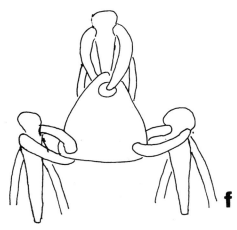

f

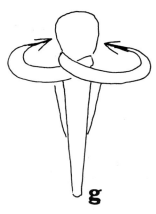

g

e. Next, cut a curved triangular base of vinyl or leather for the gourd to sit upon—not larger than the bottom width of the gourd. Force an opening in each corner for the insertion of leather strands.

f. Make a sling for the gourd by placing a long leather strand through each hole in the corner of the triangular fabric.

g. Hang the sling in the middle of the stand, crossing the respective strands around the crevice in each tent peg.

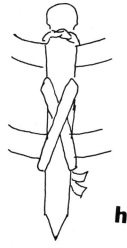

h

e

h. Continue tying the strands to the tent peg as illustrated in the drawing. Tie the ends beneath the stripping on the back of each tent peg.

The finished three-legged stand with sling is ready for the gourd to be placed inside.

Peruvian bowl from Ayacucho is embellished with a scenic panel between two decorative borders. Courtesy, Museo Nacional de la Cultura Peruana. Photographed by Seno Wilfredo Loaza

The burnt and colored gourd from the Huancayo region of Peru is decorated with three bustling scenes on three levels. Courtesy, Museo Nacional de la Cultura Peruana. Photographed by Seno Wilfredo Loaza

The burnt and carved gourd from Huancayo is decorated with a large simplistic scene of musicians and dancers. Courtesy, Museo Nacional de la Cultura Peruana. Photographed by Seno Wilfredo Loaza

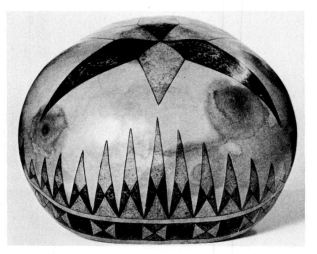

A simple, geometric pattern is burned on the surface of the triangular-shaped bowl. Larue Stith

A more complicated geometric design is burned over the gourd's surface. Larue Stith

Applied Designs and Finishes

Gourd ornamentation can be realistic, abstract, or geometric. Designs worked over the gourd may be simple or complicated, depending on the taste of the artist. On some gourds each motif has a symbolic meaning, while on others ornamentation exists purely for aesthetic reasons. The traditional and modern decoration pictured throughout this book each has its own attributes; both types of gourd ornamentation provide aesthetic enjoyment.

Many artistic methods can be learned from the artisans of Peru, Mexico, and countries of Africa, all of whom are truly experts at decorating the gourd's surface. People in those countries have lived with gourds for so long that they have worked out many excellent techniques for us. Their burnt, carved, and stained picturesque scenes and geometric designs can be seen in chapter 1 and in this chapter. Many of these gourd objects are decorated effectively using the most primitive implements. Peruvian and African techniques and tools can be used to achieve high quality work by anyone desiring to create their own decorative ornamentation on gourds.

Three of the most natural and traditional native techniques of decorating gourds are carving, burning, and dyeing. One or more of these methods may be utilized to embellish the gourd with excellent results. Burning or carving is often combined with dyeing to produce a different effect.

Carving

Carving exposes the white or light colored lining under the thin, smooth hard surface of the gourd. The depth that most gourds are carved is just slightly below the surface. The thicker the gourd wall is, the deeper the carving or engraving can be.

African gourd carving tools: curved-bladed knife, screwdriver-shaped chisel, and pointed awl.

The traditional carving tools of Peru and the countries of Africa are almost identical, even though they are located on opposite sides of the globe. Since high quality carvings are made by using these tools, perhaps you will want to fashion some of these implements yourself.

A Nigerian tool commonly used in the northeastern state is a metal screwdriver-shaped point embedded in a cornstalk handle. It is generally pulled along perpendicular to the gourd wall to make light incisions in the gourd's surface. The similar Peruvian tool for pressure-engraving is the burin, again a screwdriver-shaped chisel, but set into a wooden handle. You can make this implement by sharpening the tip of a screwdriver with the emery wheel of a Dremel Moto tool.

Another Nigerian carving tool is a curved bladed knife used by the artisans of Iwo. After the design is outlined over the gourd with the tip of the knife, deeper incisions are made and extricated from the gourd.

In Ghana a pointed tool is used to incise the surface of the gourd. The engraved lines are so fine that the Frafas rub the gourd with brown oily Shee nut so that the carving can be seen. The darkened engraving

Dr. Miller carves geometric patterns on the gourd with hand wood-carving tools, gouges, or chisels with U-shaped cutting edges. He applies dark walnut stain with a high percentage of pigment to the gourd's surface. After the carving absorbs the dark stain, he rubs the gourd with a soft cloth. For a three-color effect, stain is applied after carving part of the gourd. Then portions of the gourd are carved after applying the stain.

Carving the gourd with a U-shaped cutting gouge.

The circular designs on the gourd's surface are carved with a U-shaped gouge, then stained. Dr. Leslie Miller

The Peruvian carved and stained Sugar Bowl gourd is embellished with an everyday scene drawn from the life of the people. Courtesy, Carnegie Institute, Museum Shops

provides striking contrast with the gourd wall. When the Peruvians carve their gourds with a similar pointed implement, the engraved lines are filled with a mixture of charcoal from burnt grass and grease.

A variety of gourd carving tools are available in the United States. Small hand tools for wood carving and linoleum-block-cutting implements are obtained from craft, hardware, and hobby stores. The most inexpensive way to purchase hand tools is to buy only one handle and use the appropriate U- or V-shaped blades to fit.

Since the hard shell of the gourd is round and slippery, these tools must be handled carefully and skillfully. Always keep the hand holding the gourd out of the direct line of the blade in case the knife should slip.

Guidelines for the design may be drawn with a pencil; they can be erased before a finish is applied to the gourd wall. While following the penciled guidelines with a U- or V-shaped gouge, tilt the cutting tool at such an angle that the blade will carve just slightly beneath the surface. For safety, examine your carving position before each cut.

The safest method of carving is with a small power tool called a Dremel Moto tool. It is available at hobby and hardware stores, usually in kit form with a variety of attachments. The long pointed engraver and carver with a small ball tip can be inserted into the electric drill with ease. The only problem is that the Dremel Moto tool gets hot after a short period of use. As a result the tool must be set aside until it cools each time it is used.

Engraved areas can be allowed to remain their natural off-white color, particularly if the carving has a pleasing contrast with the coloring of the gourd wall. Often a rich appearance is achieved when both natural and stained carvings embellish the same gourd.

Staining Carved Areas

Most staining mixtures include some charcoal from varied sources. Artisans from Africa mix ground nut oil with soot (charcoal) scraped from the bottom of pans. Peruvians make ashes from burned paper or dry grass, then combine it with household grease. Another method is to pulverize a charcoal briquet with a hammer and mix the powder with peanut, linseed, or another type of oil.

Charcoal mixes for darkening carved areas are applied to the gourd by hand or with a cloth. A soft cloth or an absorbent paper towel is used to remove the excess residue from the gourd's surface.

Other products for staining incised designs are wood stains, liquid shoe polish, India ink, and dark diluted acrylic or oil paints. When using these products, the stain is applied only to carved areas and lines with a fine artist's brush. An easy way to darken incised lines is with a black or brown felt pointed tip marker having permanent color. The advantage of darkening carved lines with a paintbrush is that the gourd wall does not absorb any of the darkening agent.

When commercial stain is applied to the carved gourd, it will darken the uncarved surface slightly. However, more of the darkening agent will be absorbed by the carved areas. As a result, there will be a contrast between the gourd's smooth surface and the carving.

Burning

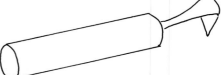

The pyro-engraving tool used in Africa is heated in a fire until it is red hot. Then the design is applied to the gourd wall with the pointed tip. Many tools are kept on the fire in order that a cool burner can be exchanged for a hot one as needed.

Pyro-engraved (burnt) bowl from Mali. After the skin is scraped from the thick gourd wall, a line design is drawn with a pointed red-hot metal-tipped tool. Courtesy, Carnegie Institute, Museum Shops

The decorative Peruvian gourd represents an Indian in a native costume who is playing a musical instrument. The black areas and shading are burned with a piece of eucalyptus wood heated over a fire. The carving is done with a burin, a screwdriver-shaped tool. Courtesy, Carnegie Institute, Museum Shops and Raquel's Collections

The intricately designed scene with motifs is burned with a heated piece of eucalyptus wood. Courtesy, Museo Nacional de la Cultura Peruana. Photographed by Seno Wilfredo Loaza

Burnt decoration enhancing the gourd can be applied without damaging the gourd wall. Versatile burning techniques employed by artists include making solid lines with a hot metal point, darkening areas of the design a solid black, and providing proper brown shading for figures, animals, and scenes.

In African countries—Nigeria and Mali—artisans decorate gourds with a "knife," a red-hot leaf-shaped pointed metal tip set into a wooden handle. The tool, measuring 14 inches, is used to draw lines over the gourd. The artists have three or four irons heating in the fire so that when one cools, another is always ready for use. Often the surface skin of the gourd is rubbed off the thick-walled gourds. When the iron is applied, the dark lines provide a beautiful contrast with the white inner layer. Burning gourds with hot irons is a method of decoration found throughout the globe—Corsica, India, other African and South American countries.

Artisans of Peru are masters of decorating gourds with four exquisite colors without artificial means. Burnt solid and shaded areas are combined with white carving, plus the natural coloring of the gourd. Shading and burning is done with a piece of eucalyptus wood heated in a fire. By blowing the stick the artist regulates the temperature to produce varied shades of brown to black.

Burning tools used in the United States are the craftsman's electrical woodburning tool, an electric soldering pen, even a child's woodburning tool. The artist's electrical wood burner with three different points can be purchased at good hardware stores and hobby shops. The tool can be used without a point for solid areas. All points tend to slip over the gourd wall while being used, but with practice the electrical wood burner is an excellent tool for decorating gourds.

American gourd artist Larue Stith achieves the elegant look of parquet flooring with two electrical woodburning tools. After deep, solid straight lines are drawn with the sharp diagonal tip of one burner, selected spaces are often filled using the circular motion of another burner having a smoothly filed tip. Other areas are filled with thin, straight lines to give the appearance of a wood surface.

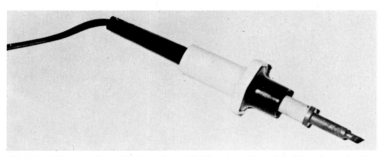

The electric woodburning tool is available at craft and hobby shops in the United States.

Burnt gourd. Larue Stith

Larue Stith achieves the elegant look of parquet flooring by using two electric woodburning tools, one with a sharp diagonal point and the other with a filed diagonal tip.

Mr. Stith says the trick to making straight lines with a burner is to measure and draw the geometric design in advance with a pencil. Establishing a visual goal from one point to another, slowly and steadily advance the tool over the penciled guide to obtain a line of even quality.

A small propane torch may be used to burn large areas. Burned areas may be contained and defined by applying two layers of masking or freezing tape over sections that are to remain the natural coloring of the gourd wall. However, the propane torch knob must not be turned on any higher than "lite." Squeeze the lighting device and ignite the torch according to the directions on the package. Once the torch is lit, keep the knob at "lite." Use a back and forth motion with the torch a couple of inches away from the gourd to scorch only the untaped areas. When the burned design is completed, remove the tape and apply one of the finishes listed in this chapter.

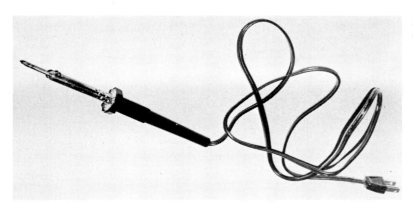

An electric soldering pen may also be used for burning.

The Swedish copper soldering tool has a tip that is turned perpendicular to the gourd wall. Courtesy, John Kraft

After drawing the design over the gourd with a pencil, Mr. Kraft fills in the spaces using the copper soldering tool. The darkness of the burn is regulated by the pressure on the copper and the temperature. The harder the pressure and higher the temperature, the darker the burn. When the decoration is completed, the pencil marks are erased with a rubber eraser, and the gourd is wiped with a soft cloth. The gourd is then finished with a neutral shoe polish. Courtesy, John Kraft

The freely decorated outlined panels of the gourd vase are burned with a Swedish copper soldering tool. John Kraft

The gourd vase and boxes are burned with a copper soldering tool. John Kraft

The uncontained dark areas of the gourd's surface are burned with a propane torch.

Starter and propane torch. The ignited propane torch may be used to burn the surface of the gourd when the knob is turned to "lite."

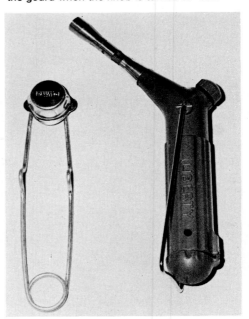

Obtaining a Mahogany Finish

Over the centuries the inhabitants of Africa obtained a mahogany finish by rubbing the gourd with oil, then darkening it over flames from a fire. The same kind of beauty is achieved by placing an oiled gourd in the oven at 200 degrees for ten-minute intervals, oiling the gourd before each baking period. This method of darkening gourds takes several days. Turning the heat higher to hasten the process will only cause the gourds to burn.

A mahogany finish may be obtained in a short time by toasting the gourd under an electric broiler. The gourd may be placed in a baking pan or pot in the best position for darkening the whole area. Allow the gourd to brown evenly by turning it with your hand covered with a heat-resistant glove.

The entire gourd may be burned with the propane torch for a mahogany finish. The burning of the gourd's surface is accomplished with the knob turned to "lite." Keep the torch a few inches away from the wall while burning the gourd with a back and forth motion.

The Leave-a-Note Box with hinged door and latch was broiled in the oven to a rich mahogany, a dark background color for the incised gold-leaf design.

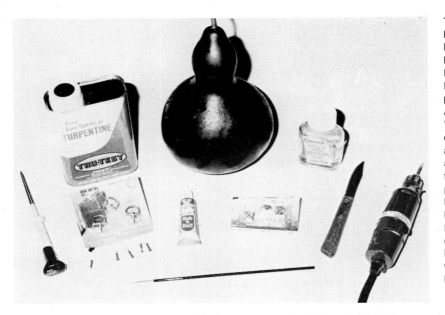

To make a similar Bottle gourd note box, you will need the following bronze-plated hardware: small hinge(s) with nuts and bolts to fit, 1″ hook and eye, a small screw-type hanging device used on wooden plaques to serve as a door handle. Artists' supplies include gold-leaf Rub 'n Buff, turpentine, linseed or cooking oil, and 00-size paintbrush. You will also need some of the following tools: a knife and handsaw, a hand-carving tool or electric engraver, awl, a pointed tool or drill for making small holes (ice pick, pointed tip of a paring knife, or the engraver of the Dremel Moto tool), a small screwdriver, and a cake pan for broiling the gourd. Use a heat-resistant glove over your hand while turning the gourd under the broiler.

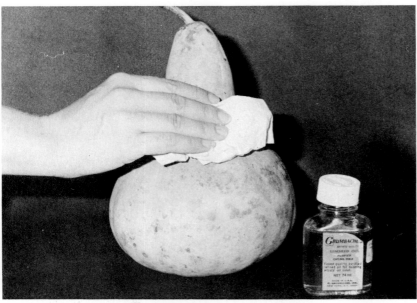

Rub oil over the gourd wall with a soft cloth.

Place the Bottle gourd in a cake pan, the long stem end over the edge of the pan. Burn the gourd under the broiler to a mahogany color, turning it as necessary to obtain an even shade.

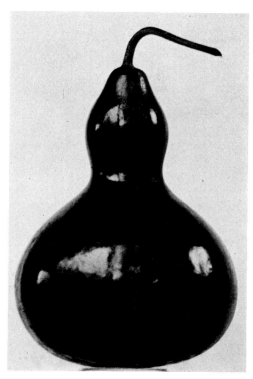

The broiled mahogany gourd is again rubbed with oil.

Draw the outline of the decoration, script, and the door with a pencil.

Fill in the incised lines with Rub 'n Buff using a fine artist's brush. To do this, squeeze a small amount of gold paste from the tube and dilute it with a few drops of turpentine. Now the gold paste can be brushed easily into the thin engraved lines.

Engrave over the penciled line of the design and script with the electrical engraver or a hand-carving tool with a narrow V-shaped gouge or an awl.

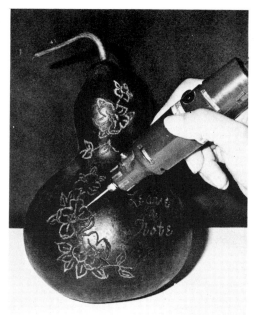

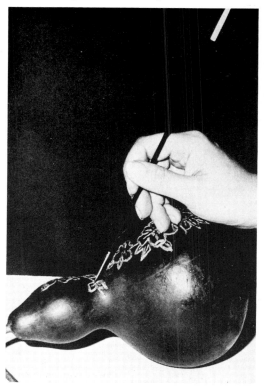

Screw the handle into the door and the latch to the adjacent wall. However, do not cut the door open yet!

Screw the latch on the right side of the door and the eye horizontally to the right of the outlined door.

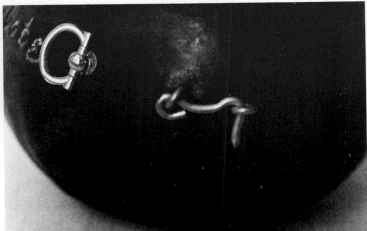

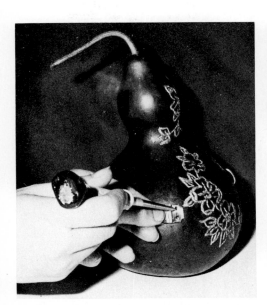

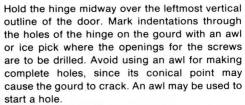

Hold the hinge midway over the leftmost vertical outline of the door. Mark indentations through the holes of the hinge on the gourd with an awl or ice pick where the openings for the screws are to be drilled. Avoid using an awl for making complete holes, since its conical point may cause the gourd to crack. An awl may be used to start a hole.

Drill the holes for the hinges through the door and window before the door is sawed. The holes may be made with an engraver or ice pick.

Cut the door open with a paring knife or saw; start the cut with a pointed tip of a paring knife.

After cleaning out the debris from inside the gourd, sand smooth the edges of the door and the open rim of the gourd.

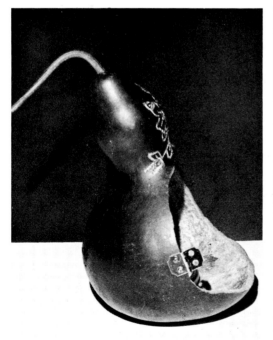

Next, attach the left side of the hinge to the gourd wall, screwing it tightly through the bolts inside. If the screws are too large for the openings in the hinges, broaden the holes with a drill using a slightly larger bit. Place the hinge so that the central pivot protrudes outward.

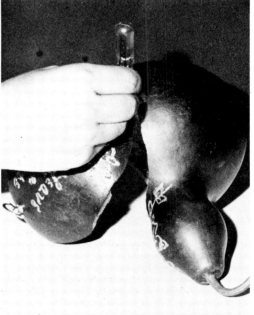

Screw the other side of the hinge to the door.

Dyeing

In Africa the natural coloring is made from stalk leaves and other natural materials. Gourds are stained indigo, red, or burnt sienna, and a further patina is achieved by constant handling. One dye is made from the red inner leaf sheaths of the Guinea cornstalk, indigo, and seedpods from the tamarind tree. After the ingredients have been boiled in water, the gourds are cooked for several hours in this liquid. Another dye is made from a paste of Guinea cornstalks boiled with cottonseed oil. The dye paste is applied to parts of the design that are to become red. Sometimes the gourd is rubbed with a concoction of millet leaves to achieve an old rose color.

Peruvian gourds are often dyed with a red or purple aniline dye. When the gourd is dry, a design is carved over the gourd wall.

Leather dye is the best and most penetrating dye that is used in the United States for coloring gourds. This dye, available in bottles at leather craft stores, must be of good quality to provide depth of color. (See Sources of Supplies.) Before using, read the precautions on the label. The dye is applied to the gourd wall by either brushing or dipping.

Because vegetable and fabric dyes do not penetrate the gourd wall easily, the most that can usually be obtained is a pale tint. Occasionally, the dye does not take at all. For tinting, add a package of vegetable dye to a quart of hot water. Keep the gourd submerged until the desired color is obtained.

A design can be made on the gourd by using a dye and the wax resist (or batiking) technique. Wax is applied to the gourd where the coloring is to remain natural, leaving the unwaxed areas free to accept the dye. See chapter 6 for illustrated directions.

Peruvian carved and burnt gourd. Courtesy, Carnegie Institute, Museum Shops and Raquel's Collections

Natural Decorating Techniques and Their Combinations

Method	Tools	Finishes
Carving	Pointed tool	Carving, leaving white layer exposed
	Curved knife	Staining carved areas and lines
	Sharp screwdriver	Dyeing, then carving
	Dremel-Moto tool	Dyeing, then staining carved areas
	Wood-carving tools	Dyeing carved green gourds
	Linoleum-block cutters	Carving and burning
Burning	Tool with hot metal tip Heated piece of eucalyptus wood	Burning the exterior surface of the gourd
	Electric wood burner	Burning a scraped gourd
	Electric soldering pen	
	Propane torch	Dyeing, then burning
	Broiling in oven	Carving and burning
	Baking in oven	
Dyeing		
Leather dyes	Dipping or brushing	Dyeing and burning
Vegetable, fabric dyes		Dyeing, then carving
Aniline dyes		Dyeing
Dyes originating from African vegetation		Dyeing carved green gourd Dyeing and wax resist Dyeing and mud resist

Lacquered box. The exquisite lacquering technique is done almost exclusively by the Mexican Olina in the mountains of Guerro. Courtesy, Mexican Folk Art Annex

Painted wine jug decanter. Courtesy, E. P. Wallace

Painting and Staining Gourds

Most paints and stains used on wood can be applied to gourds, though some have better adhesion qualities than others. Paints and coloring used on gourds include lacquer enamel, oil paints, acrylic paints, antiquing supplies, varnishes, and other wood stains. For better adhesion, gourds may be sanded before paint is applied.

LACQUER ENAMELS

For centuries lacquer enamels have been used to decorate gourds by artisans of Mexico and Central and South American countries. One Mexican method technique is begun by first lacquering the gourd with a dark background color. A design is then cut through the lacquer and the openings in the paint are rubbed with pigment using the palm of the hand.

One of the most exquisite lacquering techniques is used almost exclusively by the Mexican Olina in the mountains of Guerro. After one coat of lacquer is applied (often by dipping) and allowed to dry, a second coat of contrasting color is put on. While the second coat is still fresh, a design is incised with a tip of a thorn attached to a feather. Then a layer of earth is laid over the vessel for a period of time. When the earth is removed, it is scraped again. The entire decorative second coat stands out like a relief from the background; even elements of the design are made to stand out in the process.

Lacquer enamels are not usually available at local paint stores throughout the United States. The paints can be ordered in different colors by the quart or gallon from companies listed in the Sources of

Painted motif from a Peruvian gourd. Courtesy, Museum of Marvin Johnson

This gourd vase, painted with a flowing abstract design, has a ceramic look. The curved lines of shiny mahogany varnish provide a contrast with the dull gold acrylic paint and the white carved areas outlined with orange fluorescent paint.

Supplies. If you are planning to make any lacquered pieces, it is better to purchase paint by the gallon since it is much cheaper than by the quart.

Lacquer enamels can be ordered in flat, satin, or glossy finishes. Thinners are used according to the directions on the label. The instructions are different, depending on whether the piece is to be dipped or brushed with paint. As decoration, the paint dries dust-free, durable, and waterproof in a short time. Unlike other enamels and varnishes, it will not become soft and tacky when the weather is hot and humid.

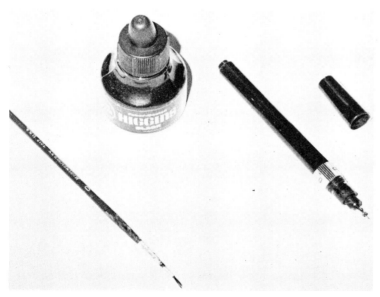

India ink, applied with a brush or pen, can also be used to add embellishment to the wall of the gourd. For smooth controlled lines, an artist's drafting pen is employed. See inked gourd in chapter 2.

The floral design on the surface of the Basketball gourd is produced by burning, carving, and painting. Carolyn Mordecai

OIL AND ACRYLIC PAINTS

Oil paints adhere more smoothly and solidly to the gourd wall than acrylic paints. Oils can be applied as decoration by using an artist's brush, or they can be applied to large solid areas with a soft cloth. A clear transparent tint is obtained by adding a few drops of linseed oil to a little paint squeezed from the tube. The thinned color is then rubbed over the gourd with a soft cloth. Turpentine is needed to clean oil paints from brushes and hands.

The first coat of acrylic paint is usually streaky, and an additional coat is needed for a solid color. Acrylics are sometimes combined with gesso and cement coloring to achieve natural earthlike colors. But when gesso is used as an undercoat for pure acrylics, a light marbleized effect is visible under the first coat of paint. The results can be seen on the mosaic-covered hanging planter in chapter 6. Because acrylics are water-based paints, water is used to thin colors and to clean the moist paint from brushes. Acrylic paints can be combined with other acrylic products to achieve many different effects.

FINISHES

Plain, undecorated Lagenarias may be sanded, then polished with a good paste wax used for wooden floors. Gourds must be waxed and polished several times to obtain a good shine. Paste wax may be used over gourds that have been decorated by burning, staining, or dyeing. Another finish is a neutral shoe polish paste that comes in a metal container.

Plastic spray and artists' acrylic medium may also be used for a protective shine. Plastic spray is particularly effective over a solidly stained gourd, for it gives the wall the appearance of polished wood. Plastic finishes may be applied over designs painted with artists' acrylics. However, do not use plastics over ornamentation done with oil paints.

Although paste wax is considered by gourd artists as the most natural finish for the Lagenaria wall, gourds are sometimes given a coat of clear lacquer, shellac, or varnish.

The geometrical design on the gourd container is carved and stained, painted, then carved again. The decorating process can be stopped permanently before each additional step after the initial carving. The problem is knowing when to stop without overworking the design.

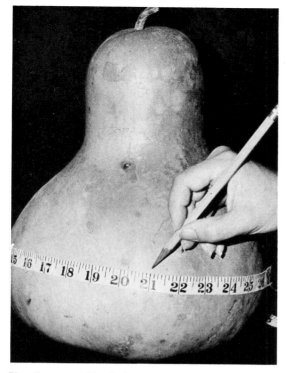

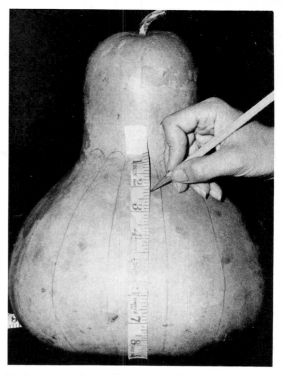

Plan the geometric design by measuring the diameter of the gourd at its broadest point. Then mark off the design widths with a pencil.

Next, measure the vertical length of the gourd from the top of the design to the bottom of the gourd. Mark off the design lengths with a pencil.

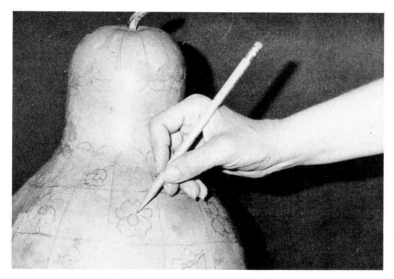

Draw the pattern over the surface of the gourd. Fill in some rectangles with circles and allow some areas to remain free from decoration. When you are finished drawing the basic design over the gourd, decide what sections are to be painted and what areas are to be carved.

Next, carve the lines that are to be stained.

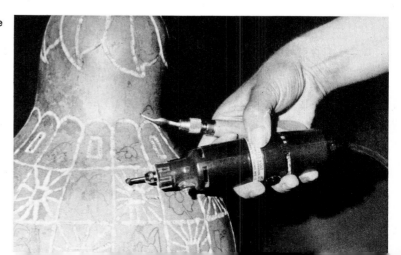

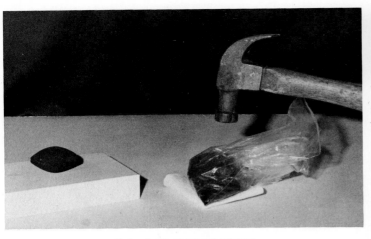

Pulverize a charcoal briquet.

Mix cooking or linseed oil and powdered charcoal to create a staining agent. If you are staining with a commercial stain, brush only the carved lines with a fine artist's brush.

Apply the charcoal mixture over the gourd allowing the residue to remain in the carving.

Stop here or go on!

Wipe the charcoal from the surface of the gourd with a clean cloth.

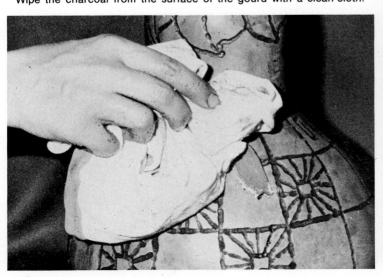

Decorating with Extraneous Materials

NATURAL MATERIALS

Small seashells, feathers, nuts, small cones, coneflowers, seeds, and a variety of other plant materials may be applied as gourd decoration. They may line the inside of gourd vessels as well as the outside. They may either be glued or wired through tiny holes in the gourd wall.

Gluing. Sobo crafts glue, Duco cement, and other glues listed in chapter 4 are good glues for adhering extraneous materials. When smooth, large materials, such as nuts, are to be glued over the gourd, it is possible to improve their adhesion by roughening the gourd wall with a sanding cylinder of a Dremel-Moto drill or other appropriate tool. Whole nuts should be baked at 250 degrees for an hour before gluing or wiring them to the gourd. This action will prevent insect infestation.

Wiring. Small nuts, seashells, and small cones may also be wired through small holes drilled in the gourd wall. Drill with an electric drill through whole nuts with a fine bit, then insert 24-gauge florist wires through the openings. Corresponding holes for the wire may be punctured through thin walls of gourd shells with a pointed tool and through thick walls with an electric drill with a fine bit.

Embedding in Wax. Mexican artisans embed seed beads to the inside wall of gourd vessels with soft beeswax. Likewise, small seeds, ornamental corn kernels, gourd seeds, minestrone soup seeds, dyed rice, and other dyed seeds can be adhered with beeswax or Sobo glue to make picturesque patterns in a gourd bowl. Small seeds can be tinted different colors in a hot concentrated solution of fabric dye or food coloring. Before applying, separate the seeds according to their types and colors into cups or muffin tins.

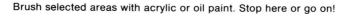

Brush selected areas with acrylic or oil paint. Stop here or go on!

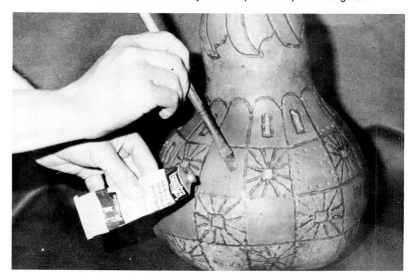

Finally, carve the inside of the circles and other parts of the design that are to remain white.

Then polish the gourd wall with several coats of paste wax. Courtesy, Johnson's Wax

Large gourds may be polished with a soft polishing disk that can be fitted onto an electric drill.

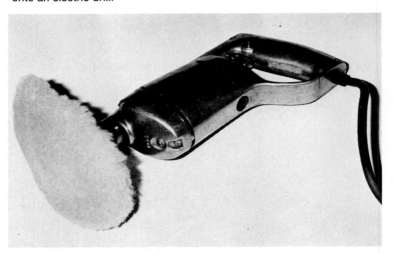

Beads may be glued to the inside of gourd vessels with Sobo glue, or else they may be embedded in beeswax. The Huichol who live in small mountain villages in Mexico decorate bowls with colorful seed bead patterns. First, the interior of the gourd container is coated with hot beeswax. In the sun and heat of the tropics the wax stays soft. The artisan presses each bead, one by one, into the soft wax. The beads are set side by side using a needle for placement until the brightly colored design is complete.

To adhere beads to the exterior surface of the gourd, first drill holes or indentations with an ice pick, drill, or small ball tip of the Dremel Moto tool. Glue the beads into the pre-drilled holes. The original African method for setting beads was to make incisions into the gourd wall. After soft clay was pressed into the incised bands, the beads were pushed, one by one, into the clay to decorate the gourd.

The Bali tribe of Cameroon encases gourds with tightly fitted seed bead coverings. Interesting gourd shapes are hidden beneath the colorful geometric patterned beadwork. In Zululand, near the southwestern tip of Africa, gourds are covered with a decorative seed bead netting. These seed beads are slightly larger than the seed beads of the American Indian.

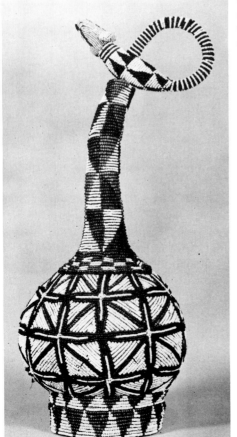

The colorful woven design of seed beads tightly encases the winding gourd used for palm wine by the Bali tribe of Cameroon. Courtesy, British Museum

Mexican seed bead bowl. The small seed beads are partially embedded on the inside of the gourd container with beeswax. Courtesy, Mexican Folk Art Annex

Embroidery. In Ghana, the Ashanti stitch pathways, a series of diagonal lines, onto darkened gourds with brass, steel, and even gold wire threads. To "embroider" a gourd, be sure an opening is cut into the gourd large enough to reach into with one hand, then drill small holes into the wall according to a preplanned design. Yarn, braid, cord, or wire is sewn through the holes with a large-eyed sewing or yarn needle.

String art is a related method for decorating gourds. Nails are driven into the gourd wall according to a preplanned pattern. The design is complete by turning yarn, braid, cord, or wire from nail to nail.

String art. The strands of jute are turned diagonally on carpet tacks, their heads protruding from the gourd wall. Courtesy, British Museum

Yarn Painting. Mexican Huichol women, known for their gourd beadwork, also decorate calabashes with bright patchworks of colored yarns. Again, the material adhering yarn to the gourds is a layer of beeswax, this time spread over the gourd's exterior surface. Stylized animals, surrounded by sections of color, are created by applying row after row of yarn over the soft wax.

Yarn, cord, or braid can also be cemented to the gourd wall with any good transparent crafts glue. In addition, yarn designs can be applied to the gourd with unadorned spaces between to purposely expose some of the gourd's surface. Yarn decor applied in this manner will stand out like a relief from the gourd wall. See the yarn tote in chapter 6.

Decorative yarn and cord such as macramé and netting make interesting coverings for gourds. Stylish slings for plain or decorated gourds and hanging planters can be made by employing the techniques of square knotting, netting, and crocheting. Beads may be added.

Weaving. Weaving may be used as a covering to protect the entire gourd. It may partially cover the gourd by providing a base for the gourd to sit on—and perhaps a handle.

In Hawaii a woven encasement hides the huge Kettle gourd beneath. Artisans of Cameroon intricately weave a decorative base with a handle. Openings in the woven design show off the darkened gourd wall. Weaving is also a means of attaching one gourd to another (see the hanging sculpture in chapter 7).

Materials for weaving may be gathered outdoors in the wilderness, or they may be purchased at craft stores selling weaving supplies. Natural weaving materials include round and flat reeds, raffia, leather strands, wood spline, cornhusks, willow, cane, jute, cattail, pine needles and cord, twisted coconut fibers, twine, cotton rope, and wool yarns. Yarns made from acrylic fibers may also be used.

Plaiting, twining, or coiling are methods of weaving that can be incorporated to add interest and embellishment to the gourd form. There are many other styles of weaving and weaving combinations.

Right:
Hawaiian baskets. A woven encasement entirely conceals the first two huge Kettle or Basket gourds; the last two gourds are covered with an open network of rope.

Below:
Gourd pitcher from Cameroon. The intricately woven partial encasement of the gourd is formed with a thick, level base and handle. Courtesy, Carnegie Institute, Museum Shops

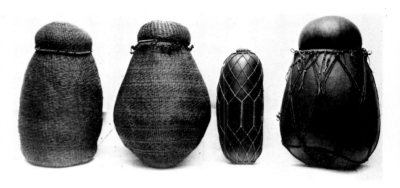

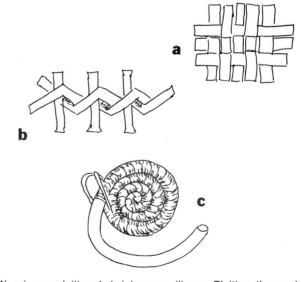

Weaving: *a.* plaiting, *b.* twining, *c.* coiling. *a.* Plaiting, the most familiar of weaving techniques, is done by passing a horizontal strand over, then under each element in a series of verticals. *b.* Twining is performed by twisting two horizontal strands around each other before passing both sides of each vertical in a series. *c.* Coiling is the circular layering of rope or wrapped bunches of grasses or pine needles. Very often, coil weaving is accomplished by sewing the top coil to the coil beneath.

The ladle, scalloped bowl, saltshakers, cornucopia, and hanging planter are all useful and practical containers for the home.

Gourd Containers

Lagenarias, Hardshelled gourds, grow into a variety of shapes and sizes that suggest their use as containers. Depending on their shapes, the gourds can be fashioned into the following items without any particular adaptations: canisters, vases, pitchers, bowls, cornucopias, strainers, dippers, sieves, jewelry boxes, waste cans, flower baskets, and other useful household objects. The photograph showing a variety of containers for the home demonstrates how different gourds are suited to their functions: the short-handled Dipper as a ladle, the large Kettle gourd as a scalloped fruit bowl, the Fish or Moranka—a cornucopia for holding nuts (cookies, candies, etc.), tiny Lagenaria bottles as shapely salt and pepper shakers, and a round Cannonball gourd as a hanging planter.

Lagenarias as Serving Dishes

People from many countries still eat stews and all types of food from gourd containers. Calabashes actually have no interior finish, except for the scraping and smoothing of the inner rind. Natives and anthropological researchers eat from gourd vessels without developing food poisoning, but those with high health standards may still wonder about the possibility of ill effects.

The gourd itself is nontoxic. When a food poisoning case is suspected, a public health official asks how long the food was left out at room temperature and not what type of container the food was in. Food left unrefrigerated for a period of time may cause illness.

Naturally the calabash should be cleaned after eating, like other dishes and utensils. Since the sanded gourd is slightly porous on the inside, you may wish to exclude some types of wet proteins (such as meat) as a simple precaution. Gourds are best used as serving dishes and canisters for dried foods (peanuts, popcorn, tea bags, beans) and for serving fruits, salads, cakes, cookies, and candies.

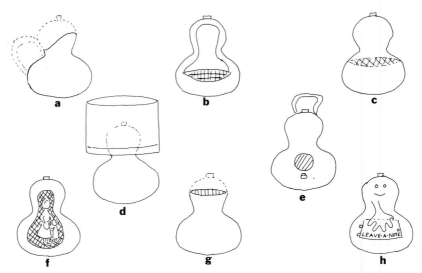

A Bottle gourd can be fashioned so that it has a number of functional uses: *a.* pitcher, *b.* basket, *c.* bowl or planter, *d.* lamp, *e.* birdhouse, *f.* panoramic gourd with scene, *g.* vase, *h.* box with hinged door.

The Penguin gourd pitcher has a burnt geometric design. Larue Stith

The hanging gourd candle rests in a leather sling suspended by two cords. Mr. and Mrs. Craig Mock. Illustrated by Gary Feuerstein. To make a similar candle, weight the wick on the bottom of the gourd container with a metal candle weight or nonflammable button. Pour melted paraffin or candle wax into the gourd as you hold the wick upright. Make a sling from leather thongs.

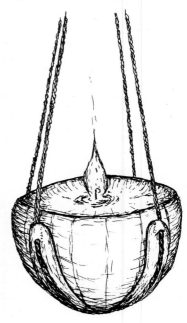

A gourd container may be cut vertically or horizontally, depending on the shape of the gourd and its intended use. Small gourds with narrow necks are cut in half lengthwise to make spoons.

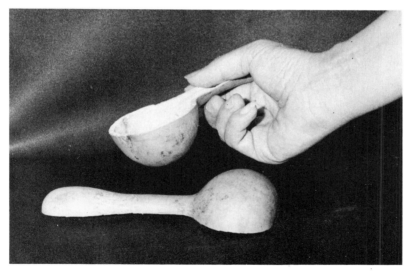

A spoon is made by cutting a small gourd with a narrow neck in half.

Creating Containers from Gourds

The charm and challenge of a gourd container is that the calabash is not perfectly symmetrical. Visual adaptations are continuously made from the beginning to the end of the crafting process. The containers are cut vertically, horizontally, sometimes even diagonally, depending on the gourd's shape and the need. Small Bottle gourds, narrow at the stem end, may be cut lengthwise to make long handled spoons.

If the container is to have a lid, the lid must be fashioned or cut so that it can easily fit into the container once again. Since a simple round lid must be turned to fit into place, the problem must be solved in some manner. One method is to extend the decoration on the gourd container onto the lid. Or else, a notch may be cut to extend from the lid's edge, which will in turn fit into the gourd container. Central and South American gourd boxes have star-shaped lids that fit into the decorative design on the calabash. A lid may have a series of rounded or pointed triangular edges, except for one point or round which is shaped differently.

When the stem is solidly intact, it can be a natural handle for the lid. Otherwise, handles may be made from other gourd parts, wood, leather, or hardware. Handles may be purchased in a variety of shapes, sizes, and finishes at hardware stores.

Both these intricately decorated calabashes from Huancavelica, Peru, have beautifully shaped lids with curving edges. The contours of the lids fit into the surface designs on the gourds. Courtesy, Museo Nacional de la Cultura Peruana. Photographed by Seno Wilfredo Loaza

To produce a box with a lid from a Canteen gourd, John Kraft cuts the stalk 1 centimeter in length. The cutting line for the lid is drawn by first placing the sharp leg of the compass into the stump of the stalk. Then the guideline is drawn around the gourd with the pencil on the other leg. The compass is also used to make guidelines for other nonfigurative ornamentation on the gourd's surface. Courtesy, John Kraft

The Peruvian carved and burnt sugar bowl has a lid that is cut to fit the design on the top of the gourd. Courtesy, Sergio Carvajal, Precolumbian Jewels

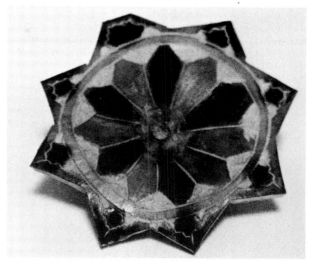

Burnt and carved Peruvian sugar bowl lid. All projections from the lid come to a point, except for one. Courtesy, Sergio Carvajal, Precolumbian Jewels

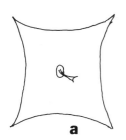
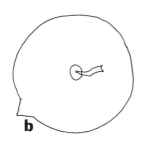

a. Four-pointed lid. b. A simple notch may be cut so that the lid will fit the container easily.

Cutting openings for gourd containers involves selecting the right tools, dependent on the strength and thickness of the gourd wall. Refer to chapter 4 for tools and methods of cutting. Here are two important cutting and sawing tips repeated from that chapter:

1. When one side of the gourd wall is thicker and tougher than the other, the amount of force exerted on the tool is naturally less for the thin wall than for the thicker one.
2. If the gourd should crack in the process, you do not have to stick with the intended shape or course of action. The new form may even be better than the original.

Should the shell be tough and difficult to cut, drill a hole in an inconspicuous place. Pour a little water into the opening to moisten the inside. Then saw the gourd according to your specifications. Avoid moistening the inside of the gourd if the lid is to be cut for the top of the container. The gourd should be completely dry when cut to prevent the lid from warping.

The following illustrations will demonstrate the basic methods used for making any type of gourd container. These step-by-step photographs show how to make a simple bowl from a large Tobacco Box gourd. The method of surface decoration is optional.

Wrap a cured gourd with a hot, wet towel until the outer crust softens—a day or less.

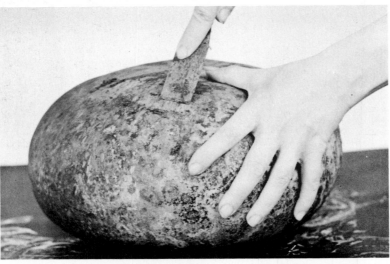

Scrape away the papery crust from the gourd wall carefully with a putty knife, kitchen knife, or stiff scrub brush.

Remove the remaining spots on the gourd under warm water with a steel wool pad. Then rinse and allow the gourd to dry.

Draw the cutting line for the opening of the container with a pencil. Since each gourd is different, use your own judgment as to where the cutting line should be.

For a smooth edge, start the opening preferably with the pointed tip of a paring or pocket knife. If the gourd wall is hard, it may be necessary to start by drilling a hole over the penciled guideline instead.

Insert the blade of a keyhole saw or X-acto saw into the cut or hole and continue to saw along the penciled guideline. If the gourd wall is soft, apply pressure over the cutting line with a pocket or paring knife until the top is freed from the container.

When the gourd is opened, the pulp with seeds can be viewed.

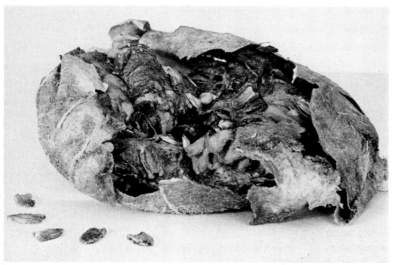

Remove the pulp and seeds from the inside of the gourds. A narrow opening at the top of the gourd may require the use of a long-handled spoon, skewer, or wire to free these materials. If the debris still clings to the gourd wall, soak the inside of the gourd with water to soften the pulp and try again.

Smooth the inside and the edge of the bowl with sandpaper. It is also a good idea to rub the exterior surface of the gourd with fine sandpaper so that when the gourd is painted or polished, the paint or wax will adhere easily.

A cylindrical sanding device on the Dremel Moto tool may be used to smooth the edge of the bowl.

The preceding directions deal with the mechanics of making a simple gourd bowl. The same basic methods are used when making other useful containers, like saltshakers, the ladle, cornucopia, and hanging planter displayed in the photograph at the beginning of this chapter. Here are short directions for creating these objects:

Saltshakers. Purchase a cork large enough to fit the entire base of each Bottle gourd shaker. Large flat bases will cause it to stand erect. To make each shaker, cut a round hole through the bottom of each gourd. Be sure that the hole is slightly smaller than the base of the cork. Clean out the pulp and seeds from the inside of the gourds. Then sand the edges of the circular openings so that the contents will not leak through later.

Drill small holes into the top of the gourds with an electric drill using a 1/16-inch bit. An ice pick may also be used for boring the holes. When finished, insert a cork in the bottom of each shaker. Cut off the bases of the corks if they extend too far from the bottom of the shakers.

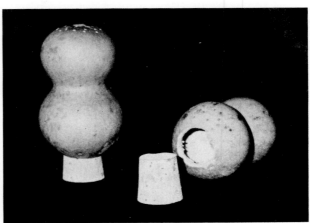

Saltshakers. A round hole is cut in the base of the Bottle gourd for the cork.

Decorative gourd vases may vary in style, color, and design. Larue Stith

Assorted gourd vases with burnt decoration. Larue Stith

Tall stately pitcher, decorated with copper coloring, stands erect on extending feet. L. S. Hartyler. Courtesy, Museum of Marvin Johnson

Cornucopia. Saw a round or scalloped opening around the broadest width of a Moranka gourd. Clean out the contents, sand the inner wall, and edge until smooth.

Dipper or Ladle. Cut a round hole in the ball of a short- or long-handled Dipper gourd. After the seeds and pulp are extracted, sand the rim and the inside wall. Insert a cork into the opening of the handle, if necessary, so that the contents will not spill into the handle.

Macramé Planter. Directions for the hanging Cannonball gourd planter are under the heading of Gourd Planters at the end of this chapter.

All the methods described in chapter 5 may be used to decorate gourd containers: natural techniques such as carving, staining, burning, or dyeing, or additional methods—appliquéing with yarns, nuts, beads, shells, and painting. The following projects are useful, decorative gourd containers that are fashioned to enhance the decor of a kitchen, living, or dining area.

Decorating the Calabash

International gourd bowl. The figures on the Kettle gourd are outlined with a wood-burning tool. Selected confined areas of the figures are brushed with light stain from the top of the can and dark wood stain from the bottom of the can. Carolyn Mordecai

To make a similar bowl with a burnt and stained design, first cut the opening in the gourd according to the directions at the beginning of this chapter. After the design is drawn over the sanded gourd with a pencil, go over the lines with a woodburning tool.

Brush the confined areas of the figures and border with stain, the lighter areas from the liquid at the top of the can and the darker areas from the thick stain at the bottom of the can.

Rub the surface of the bowl with a layer of paste wax. Courtesy, Johnson's Wax

Then polish the surface to a natural shine with a soft clean cloth or a polishing disk over an electric drill. Repeat the waxing and polishing process three or four times for a lustrous shine.

Different coloring and textured effects on the geometrically patterned bowl are achieved with woodburning tools only. See chapter 5. Larue Stith

The Nut Hut is a roomy calabash that houses the family's supply of nuts. The lid is adorned with whole nuts and walnut shells; the container is decorated with warm rust and brown stripes to match. Over the width of the gourd is a string script Nut Hut for decoration and to identify its use. Carolyn Mordecai

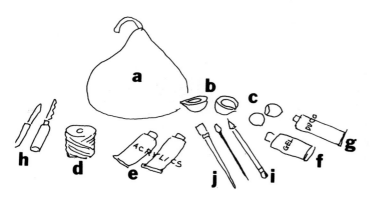

To make a nut-covered canister, you will need the following materials: *a.* Kettle, Tobacco Box, or canister-shaped gourd, *b.* empty walnut halves, *c.* whole mixed nuts baked at 250° for one hour, *d.* thick, soft string, *e.* acrylic paint and artists' brushes, *f.* plastic spray or transparent glossy medium (generally available with acrylic paints), *g.* Duco cement, *h.* keyhole or X-acto saw and pocket or paring knife, *i.* pencil, *j.* paintbrushes, Dremel Moto tool (optional).

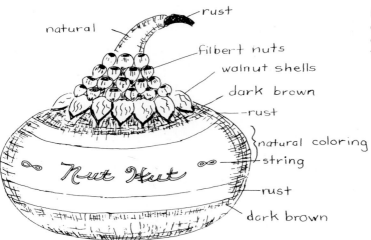

rust
natural
filbert nuts
walnut shells
dark brown
rust
natural coloring
string
rust
dark brown

Paint the stripes around the gourd with earthlike colors to match the coloring of the nuts or perhaps colors to match the color scheme of your kitchen.

1. Cut a lid with an extending notch one-third of the way down from the top of the gourd. Saw the opening according to the illustrated directions at the beginning of this chapter. 2. First cement the walnuts, side by side, around the edge of the lid allowing the tips of the shells to protrude slightly beyond the edge. 3 and 4. When dry, glue the filberts, acorns, or other nuts with pointed ends down—over and between the walnut shells. Continue by placing the nuts close together in rows above. When you get near the top of the lid, leave the tip and stem of the gourd unconcealed so that the beauty of the Lagenaria remains intact. 5. To decorate the container, draw horizontal lines around the gourd to indicate where the painted stripes will be located. Be sure to draw the outline for the widest stripe around the broadest width of the gourd. 6. Glue the words Nut Hut with string three or four times around the broadest stripe. Paint the string a bright contrasting color so that the words Nut Hut are visible. 7. As a finish, apply a protective coat of glossy medium or plastic spray.

The Yarn Tote is a spacious yarn-painted gourd that stores yarns and needles for crocheting, knitting, or needlepoint. The colorful crooked-necked gourd, featuring a lion's head, is decorated with gold, orange, white, and black strands of yarn. Colored areas of the design are outlined with black yarn. Pathways between the sections of yarn remain uncovered in order to view the natural shell of the gourd. Carolyn Mordecai

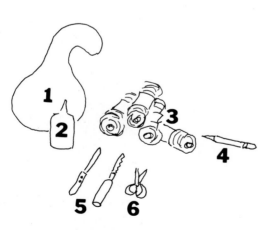

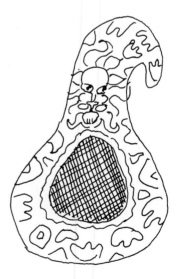

To make a similar tote, you will need the following materials: *1.* a large crooked-necked gourd, *2.* Bond's liquid cement, Sobo or Elmer's glue, *3.* 4-ply yarn in three or four colors (Use black, navy, or dark brown for outlining the design), *4.* pencil, *5.* knives, *6.* scissors.

After sawing an opening through the broad part of the gourd according to the directions at the beginning of this chapter, draw a simplistic design with a focal point or center of attraction over the gourd's surface.

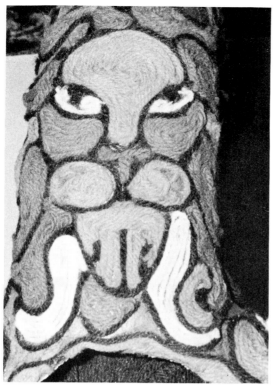

The focal point or center of attraction is a lion's head.

Glue a strand of the darkest color directly over each outline.

Start filling each section by gluing a strand of yarn next to the dark outline. Work in a circular fashion inward until the section is filled.

Add interest by having adjacent areas that contrast in color; repeat the same colors in different sections throughout the entire design. Use your lightest and brightest colors to accent small areas of the design.

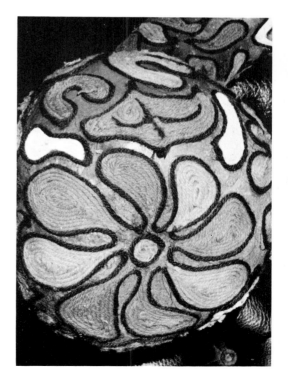

Organic seed platter. The inside wall of the gourd platter is covered with an abstract design made from red, white, and black beans, plus yellow corn. The seeds are obtained from a packet of dried minestrone soup mix. The beans and corn are also packaged separately in cellophane bags at the grocery store. An additional source of colorful seeds for decorating platters is the natural-food store.

To make an organic seed platter, divide the seeds in a muffin tin according to the color and type. Draw a simple design on the inside of the bowl with a pointed felt-tipped marker. Glue the seeds onto the platter with Sobo, Bond's, or Elmer's glue.

For a glossy protective finish, spray the platter with two coats of clear plastic.

Variation: The interior design of the gourd bowl is outlined with dark braid. The spaces are filled with colored gravel stones using white glue as the adhesive.

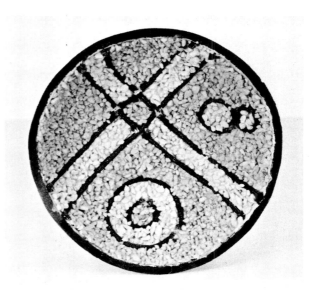

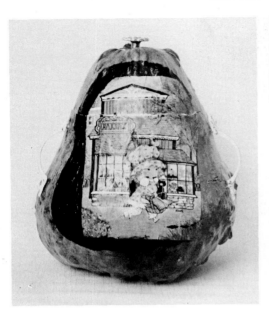

Decoupaged cookie jar. The double-handled decoupage cookie jar is mounted with a colorful print of a bake shop, its windows filled with goodies to entice passersby. The print is cemented, then covered with a fast-setting adhesive and finish called Mod Podge. This product can be purchased at most craft stores.

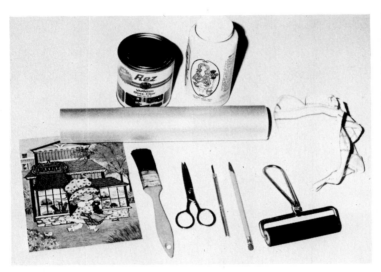

To make a decoupaged container, you will need many of the following supplies *(front row from left to right):* print, paintbrush, scissors, X-acto knife (optional), pencil, bayer (optional), rag; *(back row):* wax paper, varnish (optional), Mod Podge.

Start by brushing a coat of Mod Podge over the entire surface of the gourd.

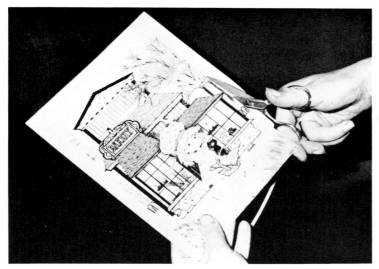

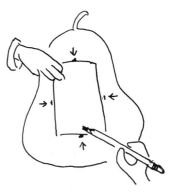

Cut the print carefully around the edge with a scissors.

After determining the location of the print on the gourd, mark light guidelines on the gourd near the print's edge with a pencil.

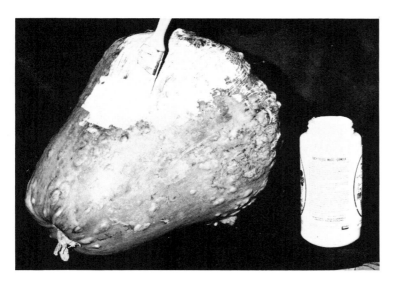

Apply another coat of Mod Podge on the gourd wall where the print is to be placed. Then quickly adhere the print to the gourd wall.

Cover the print with wax paper; roll the print with a bayer (or water glass) from the center of the print out to the edges.

119

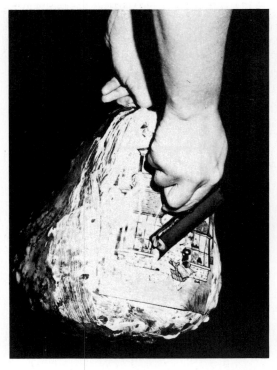

If necessary, roll out any air bubbles that remain under the print with a bayer or water glass.

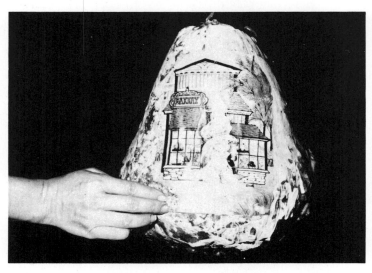

Push down the edges of the print with your fingers. Be sure that every part of the print adheres to the gourd wall.

When dry, apply a second coat of Mod Podge over the print. Brush the print from the center out to avoid buildup around the edges. Allow the coat to dry again to a clear shine.

120

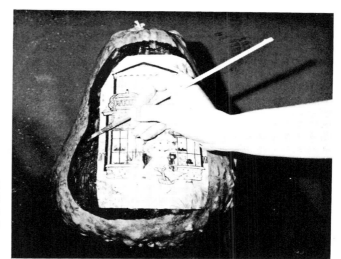

Extra coats of Mod Podge and painting the frame around the print are optional. To waterproof, brush a protective coat of varnish over the entire gourd and print.

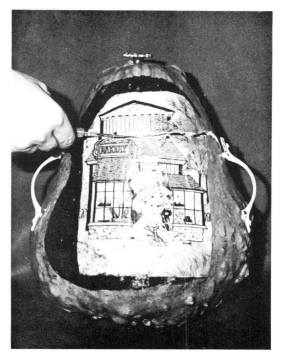

Cut the lid from the cookie jar according to the directions at the beginning of the chapter.

Optional hardware includes three drawer handles: *a.* a bridge-type handle for both sides of the jar, and *b.* a small handle for the lid. You may have to replace the original screws with smaller screws that fit completely into the holes in the handles. *c.* Washers are used over the *d.* screws on the inside of the gourd to keep the handles in place.

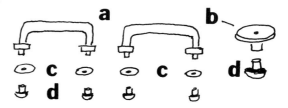

BATIKING THE CALABASH

The wax-and-dye process of batiking is generally known by craftspeople as a hand method for making colorful designs on fabric. The waxing of the material is accomplished by using a brush or tjanting tool. The tjanting tool, a wood-handled instrument, has a ball-shaped metal container with a spout for pouring the wax. Areas that are waxed remain the original color while uncoated sections are free to receive the dye coloring.

Batiking, or the wax resist process, is an extraordinary method for decorating gourds because the results are unpredictably interesting, and it is easy to do. The wax can be applied to the gourd wall in three different ways: warm wax rolled and applied by hand, with brushes, or with a tjanting tool used for fabrics.

The first is a hand method for batiking that originated in Africa. The technique is used on gift boxes made from camels' stomachs. The natives form long, thin wax threads in the hot, tropical sun. Then they press the wax into unplanned patterns on the box. After waxing, the box is dyed red, a dye from the stalks of sorgo. The box is redyed several times until the desired color is obtained. Finally, the wax is scraped from the box with fingernails.

It is possible to batik gourds in the same manner by softening beeswax in the hot summer or tropical sun. Next roll the soft, warm wax into long strands and apply it into designs over the gourd. Then dip the gourd in leather dye or brush the dye over the gourd. Remove the wax with a dull knife or fingernail.

The Bambaula camel box from Agades, Niger, is a gift box made from a camel's stomach. The line decoration is applied using a wax-resist technique of dyeing. The same wax-resist method may also be used to embellish a gourd. Courtesy, Carnegie Institute, Museum Shops

A triangular camel box with a geometric pattern is decorated using the wax-resist technique of dyeing. Courtesy, Carnegie Institute, Museum Shops

To decorate the gourd's surface using the African wax-resist method, warm beeswax in the hot sun during the summer months. 1. Roll the wax into long threads about ⅛ inch thick. 2. Apply the wax threads in a pattern on the gourd, leaving small spaces between the threads to receive the dye. 3. Dip the gourd in leather dye or brush the dye over the entire surface. 4. Remove the wax with your fingernail or a dull knife.

Batiked Bottle gourd container.

Brushing and tjanting methods of batiking are very rewarding and take less time than carving or burning. However, the process requires forethought for good results, especially when more than one color is applied. When two or more colors are involved, colors are applied in succession from light to dark.

To batik gourds, you will need a good leather dye and beeswax or an inexpensive batiking wax composed of beeswax and paraffin. Have at least two different size artist's brushes for applying the melted wax to the gourd. Tjanting tools are generally available at crafts stores with three different size ball containers and pouring spouts. Choose one. You have the option of using only brushes with the wax, or just a tjanting tool, but for variety use both. With a tjanting tool you will obtain thin, continuous controlled lines. When the tool is pulled away from the gourd, a few drops of wax will fall and add to the design. Using a brush will result in broader extensive strokes, especially applicable for filling broad areas of the design.

The batiked basket and lid are made using the wax-resist process of dyeing in which brushing and tjanting techniques are employed. The basic container is a large Kettle gourd decorated with flowers that are waxed with a brush. The lid is one-half of a broad Canteen gourd topped by a half Bottle. The continuous intersecting controlled lines on the bottom of the lid and between the flowers on the Kettle are the result of waxing with a tjanting tool. Carolyn Mordecai

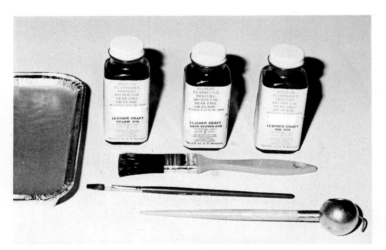

The materials needed to make a similar batiked basket include a batiking wax made of paraffin and beeswax, a tjanting tool (optional), large and small artists' brushes, good leather dye, thin florist's wire for sewing the Bottle gourd onto the Canteen gourd, dull kitchen knife or putty knife for removing the wax from the gourd's surface. Other household items include a double boiler and rubber gloves.

Melt the wax in a double boiler.

Draw this pattern or sketch your own design lightly over the gourd with a pencil. Decide what areas of the design should be waxed to keep the natural gourd coloring. Then determine what sections of the design should remain free to receive the first dye. If a second dye is to be used later, the second dye should be at least a shade darker than the first dye.

Brushing. After the wax is melted, dip the brush into a hot wax and quickly apply it to the petaled flowers on the gourd. Brush the wax on all areas and lines you wish to remain the natural color of the gourd.

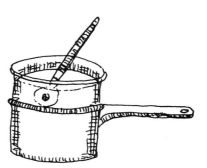

Tjanting. The thin long continuous lines on the base of the lid and between the flowers on the Kettle gourd are made with a tjanting tool. To use the tjanting tool, first fill the ball of the tool with melted wax from the top pan of the double boiler. Apply the wax by pulling the pouring spout over the outside of the gourd. The pouring spout should be in contact with the gourd to obtain long, continuous lines. The few drops formed over the gourd by lifting the tjanting tool will add interest to the batiked design.

Dyeing. If the gourd is small, dip it into a container filled with dye. Coloring is received on the large gourd by brushing the dye over the surface. When only one dye is employed, the wax is removed as the next and final step.

Optional: When a second dye is to be used, decide what areas are to remain the first dye color. Then coat sections of the first dye with wax to retain the particular color of the initial dye. Note that the unwaxed portions are free to again receive the dye. Next, brush the gourd's surface with the second dye.

When finished, dip or brush the gourd with the second dye color. The use of two dyes means that the finished design will have three colors: the natural color of the gourd wall, plus the lighter and darker dyes. Additional dyes may be applied using the waxing and dyeing methods above until the desired effect is obtained.

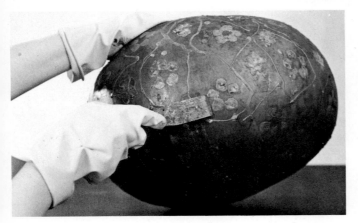

To uncover the beautiful colors that appear to get lost during the waxing process, remove the wax with a dull knife or putty knife. It is particularly easy to remove the wax outdoors under a hot summer sun.

The remaining melted wax should be cleaned from the warm double boiler with a paper towel. Do not pour the extra wax in the sink for it will clog the drain.

Gourd Planters

Gourd planters filled with nature's greenery enliven household decor inside and out. They may be suspended from the ceiling or patio roof, or rest on a table. By selecting live plants that will thrive well in desired locations, you will be able to enjoy them for a long time. Some plants require full sun, while others need partial sun or shade. Those that grow well in the sun are cactus, marigold, petunia, zinnia, sweet alyssum, Chinese juniper, and winged pea. Plants that need sunlight for only short periods of the day are asparagus fern, coleus, begonia, fuchsia, ivy, impatiens, pansy, philodendron, spider plant, and primrose. They can be used in gourd planters partially shielded from the sun by a patio overhang. Baby's tears, ferns, Swedish ivy, wandering Jew, and bridal veil will thrive in the shade.

Familiar hardy indoor houseplants are the corn plant, philodendron, snake plant, fatsia, jade plant, dumb cane, air fern, pathos, and Mexican breadfruit plant. Soil requirements vary with different plants.

Any type or shape of Lagenaria can be cut open and used as a planter. To waterproof the inside of a planter, coat the inner wall with melted paraffin. Or else line the inside of the gourd with aluminum foil.

The gourd lampshade with a light bulb inside has a plant suspended from its base. Courtesy, John Kraft

The calabash window box is filled with coleus. The gourd was grown on a board in order to provide a level base for the planter.

Table Planters. These are usually made from gourds that have flat bases. Though many gourds naturally have level bases, others must be encouraged to grow flat on one side by placing them on boards while they are growing.

A dramatic way to show off your planter is to place it on a pedestal that will sit on a table. A dowel is glued into a block of wood used as a base, then the gourd is fitted over the tip of the dowel.

Hanging Planters. To hang a planter, make a sling from jute, cord, rope, or leather strands. Slings are made using simple braiding, knotting, or crocheting techniques. Hardware chain and hooks made for hanging plants may also be purchased at hardware or variety stores.

The mosaic planter is a hanging Bottle-shaped gourd that derives its sectional mosaic effect from the combination of string, plus blue and green acrylic paints. The glassy appearance is achieved with an undercoating of gesso beneath the paint and a coat of glossy medium or plastic spray over the paint.

To make a similar mosaic planter, you will need the following materials: gesso, artist's paintbrush, string, glue, Bottle or other shaped gourd, paring knife or handsaw, long strand of leather, gel medium or plastic spray, tubes of colored acrylic paints. A drill, tip of a paring knife, or other pointed tool is useful for making holes through the top of the gourd for the leather strand. Sobo, Bond's, or Elmer's glue is used for applying the string to the gourd wall.

Cut one or more openings in the gourd wall large enough to give the plant exposure to the sun and room for growth. Use the cutting and sawing directions given at the beginning of this chapter.

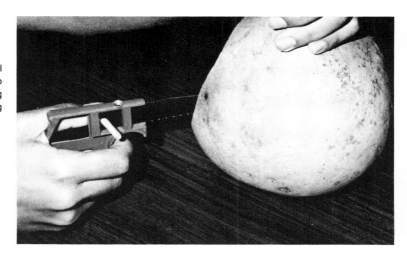

Glue a sectional mosaic pattern of string over the entire wall of the gourd.

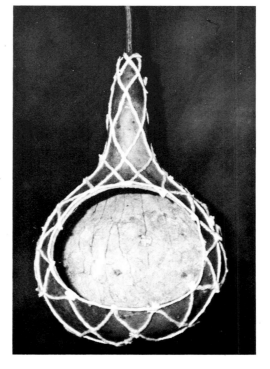

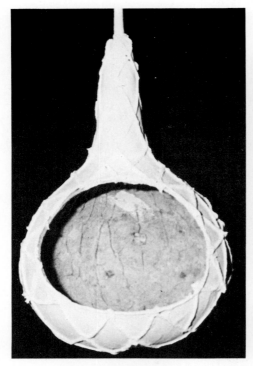

Brush a coating of gesso liberally over the string and the surface of the gourd. The gesso will harden the string and provide a light-colored surface under the acrylic paints.

Paint sections between the string with acrylic paints making adjacent areas each a different color wherever possible. Leave the string white, as shown here, or else paint it with a contrasting color.

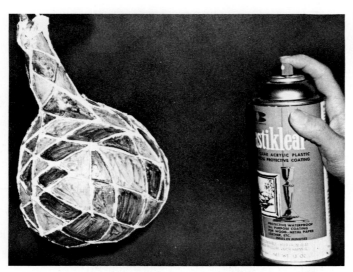

For a protective shine, brush the mosaic planter with a coat of glossy medium or spray it with one or two coats of plastic spray.

Melt paraffin in a double boiler.

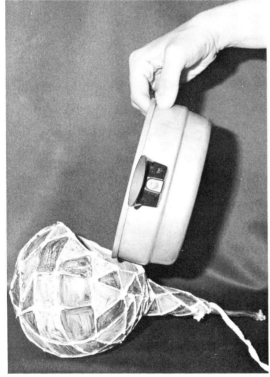

Waterproof the planter by pouring the melted paraffin inside and rolling it over the interior wall.

After drilling holes through the top of the gourd, insert the tip of a leather strand and form a knot.

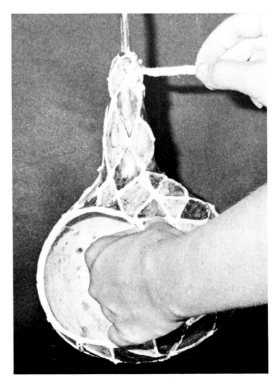

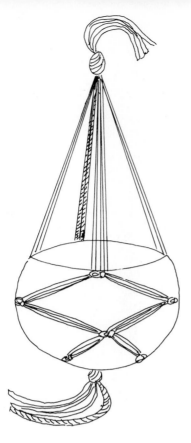

A gourd planter with a simple macramé sling.

1. Using jute or other macramé cord, cut 8 strands two or more yards in length for a 6–7-inch planter. Align the strands evenly. Tie an overhead knot at one end, leaving a tassel of at least 7 inches.

2. Divide the strands into four equal groups with 4 strands in each. Tie a complete square knot from each group a couple of inches from the sling knot. Use knotting Method I or II:

7"

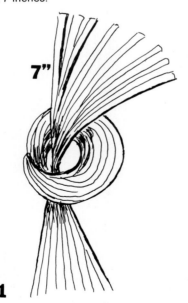

1

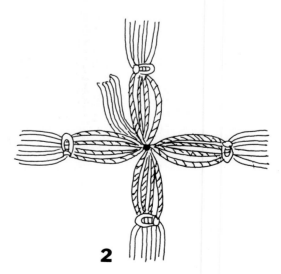

2

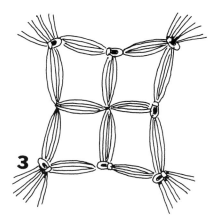

3. Make four more macramé knots using adjacent cords from each group: two cords from one group and two cords from the next. Form the four square knots a couple more inches from the first knots.

Place the sling under the gourd planter. Alternate to the original groups of four, tying four more macramé knots a few inches beyond the second row of knots. Tighten the row of knots close to the planter to make a pocket that fits. If the pocket is not large enough, alternate to the adjacent cord and knot the groups of four in the same manner as before. Finish by tying another overhead knot at the top of the sling. Cut off excess cord from the tassel. (See original drawing of planter and the photograph of gourd containers at the beginning of the chapter.)

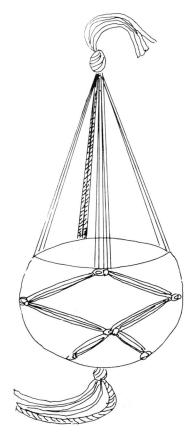

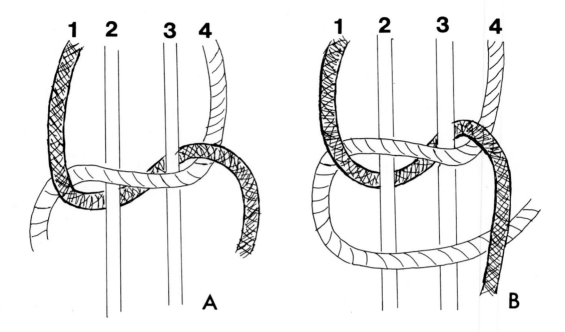

Macramé knot—Method I (the most popular method)

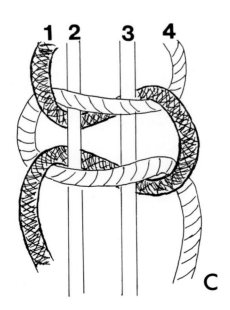

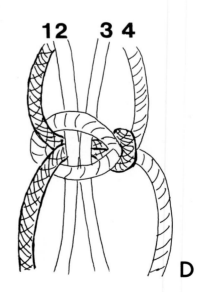

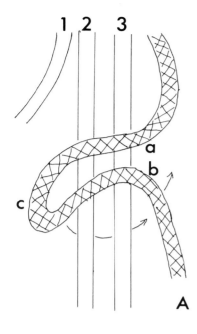

Macramé knot—Method II

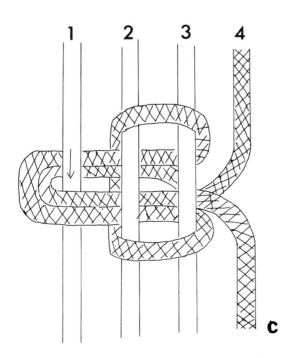

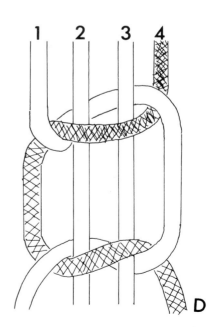

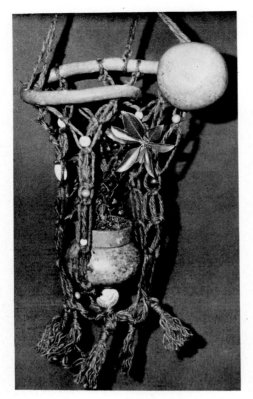

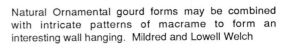

Natural Ornamental gourd forms may be combined with intricate patterns of macrame to form an interesting wall hanging. Mildred and Lowell Welch

From holes in the curved handle of the Dipper gourd is suspended a patterned macrame netting that is gradually shaped to form a sling for holding the gourd planter. The ends of jute at the bottom of the net are tied into tassels.

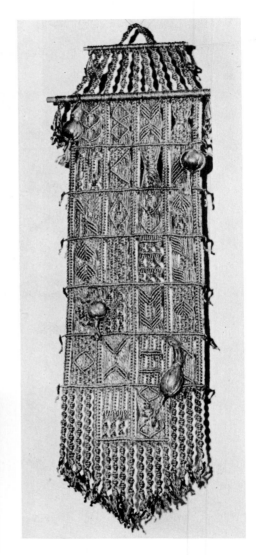

Gourd and Macrame wall hanging. Minnie Black.

Macrame techniques may be used to make decorative slings to display the surface decoration of whole gourds. Decorated gourds Dr. Leslie Miller
Courtesy, Museum of Marvin Johnson

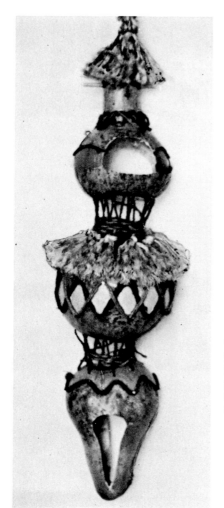

Triple gourd hanging.   Three Lagenarias, woven together, are decorated with strands of jute running from nail to nail. Areas between the jute outlines are painted with bright acrylic paints. The upper and middle gourds are topped with combed fibers of Manila rope.

The sculptured vase is made from carved and painted Penguin and Bottle Lagenaria. It has three Ornamental Pear gourd spouts at the top. Carolyn Mordecai

To create a similar sculpture, you will need a variety of different shaped gourds, plus the following materials: a hand-carving tool or Dremel Moto tool with ball-tipped engraver, plastic wood, Duco cement, artist's paint-brush small enough to fit in carved grooves, oil, and cotton. Masking tape is also used to hold gourd parts together during the sculpting process. In addition, have handy a pencil and paper for planning the balanced form of the sculpture and its decoration.

After preplanning the shape of your sculpture from all angles, boldly cut out round sections from each gourd so that they will all fit together later. A gourd may have as many as three openings, such as the gourd used as the base for the sculpture shown here.

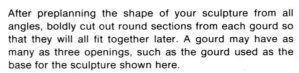

Sculptural Forms

Gourd Sculptures

A freestanding gourd sculpture receives beauty from its form in space, its smooth or warty texture, and added embellishment. A single well-shaped gourd, placed on a board or pedestal, may be a sculpture in itself. Other gourd sculptures, realistic or abstract, may be composed of a number of carefully selected Lagenaria and Ornamental gourds.

An artistic gourd sculpture is made by boldly cutting gourds from their original shapes into new forms that fit together. After the gourds are combined into a three-dimensional form, one is not always aware that a Spoon, Penguin, or other type of gourd is involved. The whole actually becomes more important than the parts.

The ideal sculpture looks well from any vantage point. Since working with three-dimensional forms requires forethought, it is important to draw your preconceived ideas on paper first—the back and front views at least. Planning your strategy step by step in advance will ensure more accurate results. But feel free to change the structure as you progress to achieve good form.

Sculptures are made by utilizing the methods described in chapter 4. Their parts are combined by gluing, sewing, weaving, and nailing with the use of Sculptamold. Usually, gourd shapes are stained and decorated before they are put together, but not always. The bottom of the gourd sculpture may be weighted with plaster of Paris or with stones or fishing weights in Sculptamold paste.

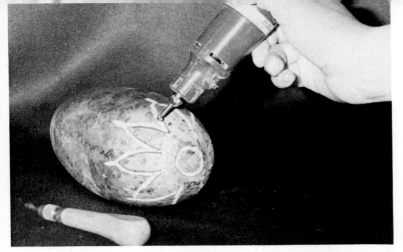

After planning in advance where the decorative motifs will be on each gourd of the sculpture, carve the design into each gourd with a hand-carving tool or Dremel Moto tool.

Fit the gourds together into a balanced sculptural form according to the original plan. If necessary, cut the openings again for a better fit.

Brush the carved outlines of the design with dark paint and selected areas of the design with bright color(s).

When you are certain that the gourds fit together well, permanently combine the sculptural parts by starting with the first two gourds at the base of the sculpture. Hold the two gourds together with masking tape. Then soak a length of cotton in Duco cement and place the moist cotton over the joint. Be sure to completely surround the joint with lengths of glue-soaked cotton. Combine the remaining gourd forms of the sculpture from the bottom up by adhering the parts in the same manner.

When dry, cover each joint with a layer of plastic wood. After the sculpture is finished and the plastic wood has hardened, paint the plastic wood, if necessary, to blend with the coloring of the gourds.

Soft-sculptured vase. A soft sculpture with three open spouts is attached to the opening of the stained warty gourd. Multicolored yarn is wound over the soft rope using a coil method of weaving.

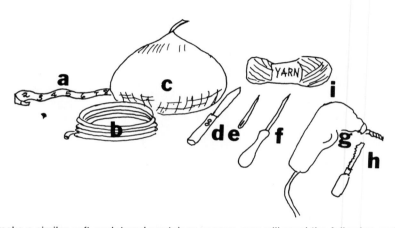

To make a similar soft-sculptured container or vase, you will need the following materials: *a.* measuring tape, *b.* clothesline or soft camping rope, *c.* gourd, *d.* paring knife, *e.* yarn needle, *f.* awl, *g.* electric drill (optional), *h.* handsaw or pointed paring knife, *i.* yarn.

a. Saw off the top of the gourd according to the directions at the beginning of the chapter.

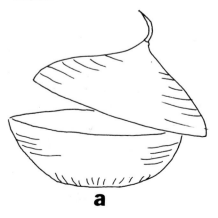

a

b. Indicate where the holes are to be drilled with a pencil—approximately ½ inch apart.

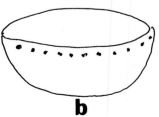

b

Indent the marks with the awl or another pointed tool to facilitate the drilling of the holes.

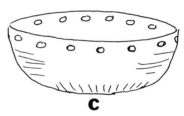

c. Drill holes through the indentations around the edge of the gourd.

d. Stain the gourd with a wood stain, which will blend with the coloring of the yarn (optional).

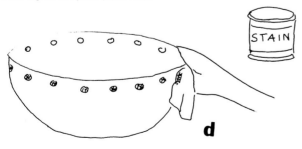

e. Thread the needle with one yard of yarn at a time. Start the coil weaving by first layering the end section of rope over the rim of the gourd bowl. Then lay ½-inch tip of yarn over the rope. Press the end of the yarn over the rope as you bring the needle over the outside and through the hole in the gourd.

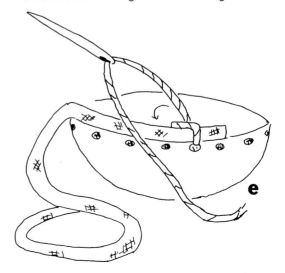

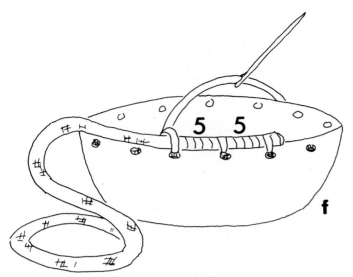

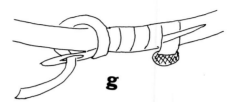

f. Pull the yarn up over the back of the rope. Encircle the rope with yarn five times, while hiding the end of yarn in the process. After winding the yarn the fifth time, push the needle through the next hole in the gourd from the outside in. Continue weaving the rope to the rim of the gourd until the circle is complete.

g. When the yarn threaded to the needle is almost used up, insert the needle next to the rope back through the coil weaving. Pull the yarn through tightly. Continue weaving with the yarn in the same manner until you arrive at the second row.

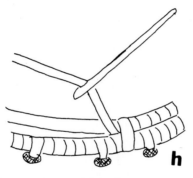

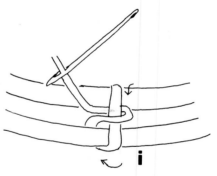

h. At the beginning of the second row, wind the top rope five times, as usual, and pick up the rope beneath.

i. To do this, bring the yarn needle toward you, then under the bottom rope. Next, pull the yarn to the right—over and under the vertical attachment. After winding five to six times, weave the yarn to the rope below at ½-inch intervals. Lay the top rope over the rope below in such a manner that the shape of the finished product will meet with your specifications.

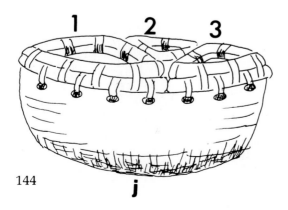

144

j. To make a triple opening, such as in the sculptured vase, weave the first row around the entire rim of the gourd, as directed. Notice that the cylindrical spouts start with three circles of rope—small, medium, and large. Weave each cylinder separately, attaching the next row to the one below wherever possible.

The shiny mahogany gourd sculpture is a combination of smooth and warty Lagenaria attached by multicolored coil-woven cylinders. Long strands of rope threaded in and out of the gourds establish the interesting lines from the top to the bottom of the sculpture. Rows of yarn are simply glued onto the bottom gourd.

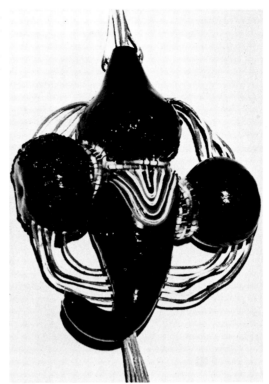

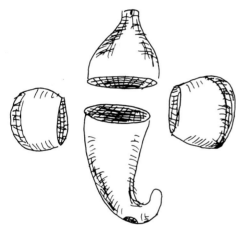

To make a similar sculpture from gourds, select the types of Lagenaria to be used. Then draw a preliminary sketch of the sculptured form. Keep in mind that an opening will be cut in each gourd large enough to put your hand into during the weaving process. For a similar sculpture, generally follow the steps and methods used to make this hanging coiled sculpture.

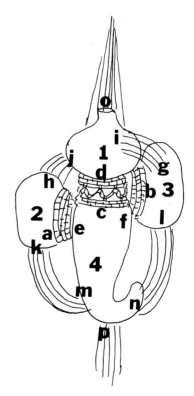

The large openings *a, b, c,* and *d* are cut in the gourds for the solid weaving. Drill a series of small holes ½ inch apart around the large openings according to the directions *b* and *c* of the preceding project, the soft-sculptured bowl. Start the holes with an awl and finish them with a drill. Next, drill a corresponding series of holes at *d, e,* and *f* to attach to coil weaving. Gourd walls *g-i, j-h, k-m,* and *l-n* will each need a set of five holes for the strands of rope on both sides. In addition, a hole is drilled on both sides of opening *o* for a single strand of rope. An opening *p* at the bottom is large enough for all ten ropes to go through. The best time to stain or paint the gourds is after all the openings are cut and the holes are drilled.

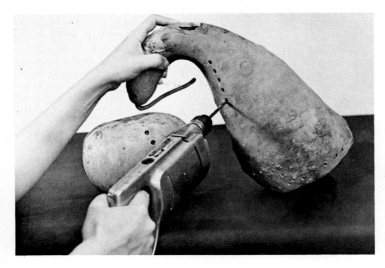

A set of five holes being drilled.

Weave several rows of coils onto the large opening of each gourd (1, 2, 3, 4). Use the step-by-step directions for coil weaving (e, f, g, h, i) the soft-sculptured bowl on pages 143 and 144. See drawing at bottom of page 145.

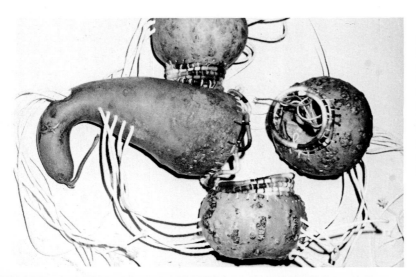

Before sewing the coiled gourds together, insert the series of painted or unpainted ropes through the series of holes on each side of the sculpture according to plan. Start by inserting the ten ropes through the openings at the top and proceed downward, half the strands on one side and half the strands on the other.

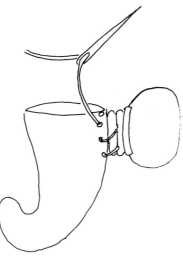

Combine the gourds into the sculpture by sewing the last row of weaving to the corresponding gourds (a to e, f to b) and last of all (d to c). Again, refer to the drawing on page 145.

When finished, pull the rope into the shape and proportions to fit the sculpture. Refer to your sketch of the original plan. Then tie a slipknot at the top extending ends of the rope.

Optional: Painting or staining of the gourd is accomplished easily before the coils are woven into the gourds. If you decide that the gourds need a paint job at this time, brush the paint over each gourd carefully. Use a small brush near the coil-woven areas.

Finally, add color to the bottom gourd by applying a series of yarn strands with Elmer's glue.

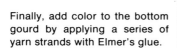
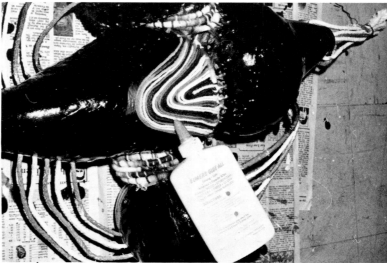

The bright colored double-faced clown, happy on one side and sad on the other, is made from a Bottle gourd. It has two small Pear gourds for noses. The ball at the tip of the hat, the rim of the hat, and the mouth are made with Sculptamold paste.

To make a similar clown, you will need the following materials: two small Pear or Spoon gourds, one Bottle gourd, Sculptamold (crafts store), small carpet tacks, Sobo or Elmer's glue, acrylic paints, paintbrushes, pencil, clear plastic spray or transparent glossy medium sold with acrylic paints. In addition, you will need strips of leather or yarn and a pencil for drawing on the gourd.

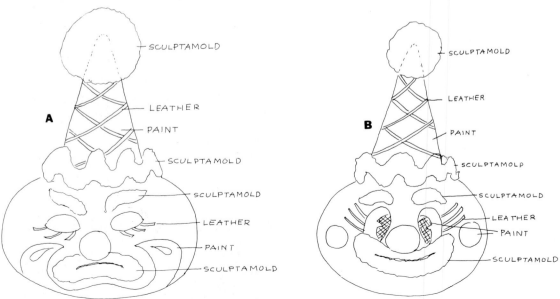

Draw the outlines for the double-faced clown on both sides of the Bottle gourd. Use patterns *A* for the sad face or *B* for the happy face or else design your own.

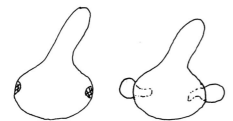

Cut out 1½- to 2-inch circles, one on each side of the gourd for the noses. Glue a Pear or Spoon gourd into each opening.

Pound carpet tacks in areas reserved for the Sculptamold: the eyelids, brim of hat, the ball at the top of the hat and the mouth. Be sure that the heads of the nails extend beyond the surface of the gourd so that they can serve as anchors for the Sculptamold.

After mixing four parts Sculptamold with three parts water, apply the paste to the mouth, eyelids, and hat. Spread the lips of the mouth apart with a handle of the spoon while the paste is still moist. Allow the face to harden on one side before adding the Sculptamold on the other. Glue diagonal crisscrossing strands of yarn or leather to form diamond shapes on the hat.

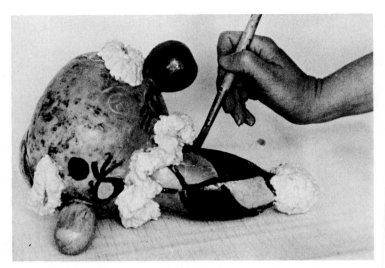

Brush each diamond with a colored paint, leaving a diamond unpainted here and there. Use two coats of paint, if necessary. Then paint the facial features on both sides of the gourd.

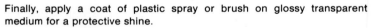

Finally, apply a coat of plastic spray or brush on glossy transparent medium for a protective shine.

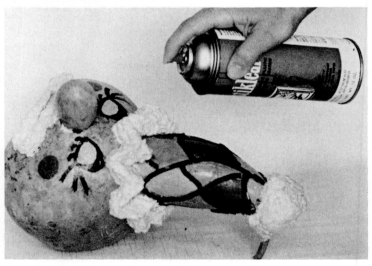

Realistic Animals and People

In the countryside near East Bernstadt, Kentucky, is Minnie Black's Gourd Craft Museum, which houses her collection of prizewinning gourd animals and people. Mrs. Black creates lifelike animals and people from the gourds she raises.

To make animals or people from cured gourds, Mrs. Black begins by selecting the shapes that best fit her project. She picks one gourd for the head, another for the arms, and others for the legs from her own stockpile of home-grown gourds. Both large and small gourds are needed.

The gourds are then cut with a knife or saw and nailed together with fine nails at the joints. After powdered Sculptamold is mixed with water until it forms a paste, it is smoothed over each joint. When dry, the Sculptamold is sanded smooth and painted a matching color.

For fine work—such as hands and feet—Mrs. Black molds clay over thin wire. The wires are inserted into small holes drilled into the gourd wall. Mrs. Black believes in creating animals and people with a realistic look. Most of the time she retains the true coloring of the gourds.

The cow and her calf are true-to-life gourd sculptures created by Minnie Black. Courtesy, Minnie Black

Self-portrait of Minnie Black, 1976. Courtesy, Minnie Black

Minnie Black's doll family. At the left is an early portrait of President Richard M. Nixon. Next to Richard M. Nixon is a self-portrait of Minnie Black. Minnie Black

The North American Indian is adorned with feathers, seed bead bands, Luffa gourd, and a chicken-neck-bone necklace. Minnie Black

George Washington. Minnie Black

Sculptural Arrangements

Gourd sculptures may be combined with flowers, greens, or other natural materials to make sculptural arrangements. They make beautiful seasonal decorations for the home or office on a desk, mantel, or table. During the spring and summer, available colorful fresh plant material may be added; in the fall and winter, dried materials may be chosen to accent the sculptural form.

A gourd arrangement may stand alone on a table or mantel, or else it may be incorporated into a larger setting with a blending background— perhaps a collage or painting. The arrangement combined with its harmonizing background becomes a total work of art. The only requirement is that the painting or collage be simple in color and design so that the arrangement becomes the focal accent in the foreground. A simple painting may inspire the style and coloring of the arrangement or vice versa. Colors and designs from the painting may be repeated effectively in the flowers and leaves accenting the sculpture, then again, the opposite may be true.

The sculptural arrangement should be planned according to how it will be viewed in its setting. When the arrangement is to be a centerpiece seen from all sides, it will have to be worked on from every angle. If the arrangement stands on a bookshelf near a wall or fireplace mantel, it is mainly worked on from the side facing the viewer.

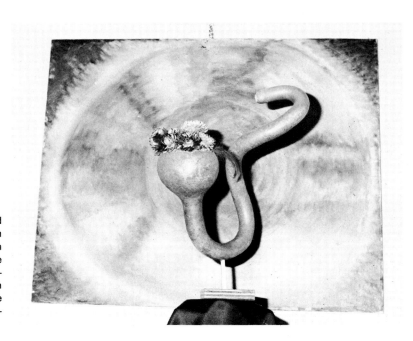

The "Pipe" is a Dipper gourd planter on a pedestal base. In the bowl of the pipe is green Styrofoam, which holds the stems of the bright dried flowers. An abstract oil painting with blending colors provides the background for the arrangement. Carolyn Mordecai

Sculptural Arrangement Techniques

Choose gourds and plant materials for color, size, texture, and shape so that when these elements are combined, they look well together. A preliminary sketch of the entire design, which includes the sculpture and added materials, will help.

Start by selecting a well-shaped single gourd or several gourds for the sculptural form. By referring to chapter 4 and reviewing the beginning of the chapter, you will find a desirable method for combining the gourds into a sculpture. Next, decide the type of base the sculpture with materials will stand on: a pedestal, caster, board, gourd base, or other. Sometimes the sculpture is weighted inside the bottom gourd and will stand alone without any support.

Choose fresh or dried materials that will accent and blend with the gourds without overpowering them. After the sculpture is attached or placed on a base, arrange plant materials in florists' holders set inconspicuously inside or near the sculptural form. As you place the materials, try to follow the lines of the sculpture without crisscrossing. Place the largest accent where the eye tends to rest—often directly beneath the tallest line. In general, place smaller flowers and greens higher and larger materials lower in the arrangement. Avoid filling each space, for unfilled, negative space is just as important as solid lines and areas. Simplicity and a well-selected minimum of materials are secrets of a good design.

Common tools and materials for arranging techniques. *Front row from left to right:* needle holder, florist's wire, clippers for cutting plant materials, long-nosed pliers with wire-cutting edges inside (the tip of the pliers is also used for twisting wires together), water pick, and nails. *Back row from left to right:* floral tape, plastic fishing tackle, Oasis, and Styrofoam.

Holders for Adding Materials

Plant materials are combined to the sculptural form or base by any means possible: nail, wire, tape, pin holders, water picks, florist's clay, or through holes or crevices in the gourds. The mechanics should be well hidden by accent or filler materials. The most useful, durable holder, which is available at a florist's or variety store, is the common pin holder. The pin holder may hold both dry and fresh materials. Some are made with a cup-shaped container beneath to hold water; others are designed so that they can be screwed to a wooden base. With the variety of pin holders available, you can select a type that best suits your need. Hint: When a stem is too thin or weak to be pushed into a pin holder, place a stronger stem or wire next to the existing stem. Then tape the stems together by winding them with matching brown or green florist's tape.

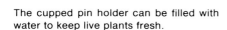
The cupped pin holder can be filled with water to keep live plants fresh.

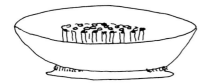

The water pick may hold a live single-stemmed floral accent or a bunch of smaller stemmed materials. The pick can be easily hidden in or behind the gourd shape.

A fresh single-stemmed-flower accent or bunches of smaller fresh materials may be inserted into water picks or test tubes. These small holders may be attached on the sculptural form or else they may be hidden through precut holes in the gourd sculpture. Live materials will also remain fresh in small containers or gourds filled with Oasis* (saturated with water). Plants may also be placed effectively near the sculpture as accent material. To place stems of dried material, you may use Styrofoam covered and wound with a layer of florist's tape. The block of taped Styrofoam may be adhered to a wooden or ceramic base with florist's clay, or it may be pushed into a presawed hole in the gourd. Dried flowers will look well if their stems are simply placed in green Styrofoam.

To attach fruit, vegetables, or food chunks to the gourd sculpture, drill holes in the gourd small enough for the placement of fondue sticks or strong toothpicks. Insert the sticks, tipped with glue, into the holes. When dry, press the fleshy parts of the fruit and vegetables, meat or cheese chunks onto the sticks; wind grapevines over the projections.

* Oasis is a green cake of foam that absorbs water. It can be purchased at a florist's shop.

Tips for Using Fresh Plant Materials

Pick flowers in the early morning or evening hours when the day is cooler so that they will not wilt. Carry a container of water outside in which to immediately place the stems. Cut the stems at a slant so that they will absorb more water.

Flowers will last longer if their stems are soaked in warm water up to their blossoms for a minimum of two hours. Better still, keep them in warm water overnight.

Keep the stems of fresh materials in water the entire time that you are arranging the materials.

To give interesting shapes to long leaves, apply a thin wire to the back of each leaf with cellophane tape. Then carefully bend the leaf to fit your design.

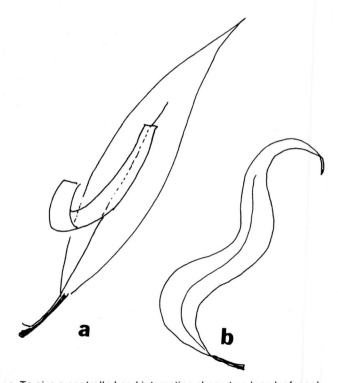

a. To give a controlled and interesting shape to a long leaf, apply a thin wire to the back of each leaf with cellophane tape. *b.* Then carefully bend the leaf into the desired shape.

Yellow-petaled flowers with black center and green leaves, plus sections of Dipper gourds, fill the sculptured gourd vase. The angular flower and stripes on the vase are painted yellow and green to match the flowers and leaves. The carved outlines of the design are painted earth brown.

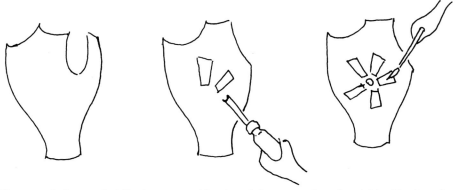

The precut stem end of the large gourd is placed down on a board or table. The broad portion at the top is opened and cut into an interesting series of shapes. This opening extends downward on one side so that the arrangement is not symmetrical. Then a simplistic design is carved and painted on the surface of the gourd.

The Dipper gourd handles are cut so that they fit into the sculptured vase.

The Dipper gourd parts are strategically placed into the vase.

After the cupped needle holder with water is placed inside the gourd vase, the cut flowers are arranged according to your taste.

Tips for Using Dried Plant Materials

The exciting dried materials used in gourd arrangements are flowers (air-dried or dried in silica gel), glycerined foliage, pods, cones, ornamental grasses, cornstalks, grains, and weeds. Many can be found along the roadside, others may be purchased at a florist's, grocery or department store.

The highest quality plant materials from outdoors are collected from early spring to late fall. By observing which plant materials stay intact during the winter months, you will become aware of the materials that will keep well in arrangements.

158

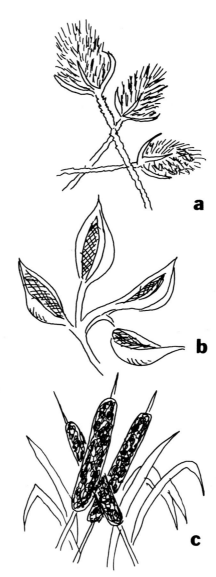

Weeds: *a*. teasels, *b*. milkweed pods, *c*. cattails.

Weeds. Along the roadside in the ugliest fields you can find patches of weeds that can be used in the most professional arrangements. Be careful that you are not picking materials in preserved lands. Take along a pair of garden gloves, clippers, and a tote bag, wear protective clothing, and you will be all set.

Common weeds that can be found in temperate climates are teasels, milkweed pods, cattails, goldenrod (green, yellow to gold as summer progresses). Others are Queen Anne's lace, cornflowers, steeplebush, seedbox, horsemint, rosehips, and sensitive fern. Cut teasels in the fall well after their lavender flowerets have bloomed. Shake the seeds from their prickly bulbs into the field before you go home.

Though it is better to cut milkweed when the pods are still green, pods picked after they have weathered can be painted and used successfully in arrangements. If fresh green milkweed is cut, open the pods and remove the seed when they are almost dry. Throw the rows of seed away immediately.

Cattails are found in swampy areas in late August and early September, well before gusts of seeds are ready to burst from their dark brown pods. Seal the elongated pods with heavy hair spray or plastic spray in the field.

The weed patch is the perfect place to shake seeds from all weeds and to spray them in order to avoid a messy situation at home. Delicate weeds, in particular, are kept intact by spraying with plastic or heavy hair spray. Dried plant materials may be left their natural colors, or they may be painted by brushing, dipping, or spraying methods. Almost any kind of paint will do; enamel, acrylic, poster, artists' oils, or casein. If one coat is too thin, apply another.

Grasses and Grain. To dry wild and ornamental grasses or grains, hang them upside down in bunches with only four to six stems in a cool, dry, dark place. For an interesting curve, stand them in an empty vase or jar.

Cornstalks and Husks. Cornstalks not dried in the field may be set upright in a container. Avoid leaning the stalks against the wall because they will dry flat on one side. To dry husks, spread them between two layers of newspapers, allowing air to circulate so that they will not mildew. The natural honey color of cornstalks and husks may be sufficient for your purpose. But if you prefer to change their coloring, they can be dyed with a ratio of a packet of fabric dye to two-thirds bucket of water. Soak them until the desired color is obtained. Husks and stalks may also be lightened by soaking them in one quart of Clorox bleach to a washtub of water.

Foliage. Beech, laurel, maple, and oak branches can be preserved by placing their stems in a solution of one part glycerin (purchased at a pharmacy) to two parts water. The stems should be split and some of the bark removed so that the solution will be absorbed easily. Stems are soaked in glycerin a few days to three weeks until the leaves change color.

A coat of plastic spray will curtail the evaporation of fresh foliage for temporary preservation. Evergreens may be preserved during the holidays in this manner.

Flowers. You can make your winter gourd arrangement bright by adding dried flowers from your garden. Everlasting flowers dry, retaining most of their natural coloring by simply hanging them in bunches in a warm, dry place. Such flowers are the strawflower, sea lavender, everlastings, statice, globe thistle, money plant *(Lunaria)*, *Gomphrena,* and Chinese lantern.

Many beautiful flowers dry well embedded in boxes of silica gel (purchased at florists' by other brand names). Such flowers are delphiniums, roses, and zinnias. They may be preserved for arrangements in three stages: bud, one-half full, and open. Cut the flowers after the sun has dried the dew; keep the flowers fresh by placing their stems in water while picking. Should the flowers wilt, revive them by placing their stems in warm water. Embed the flowers as soon as possible in silica gel according to the directions on the label.

A single-stemmed Dipper gourd vase requires only a minimum of dried materials. Two eucalyptus stems are used to establish the S-shaped line; the single dried flower in the middle serves as an accent or focal point of the design.

To make a similar arrangement, drill or cut a hole into the handle of the Dipper gourd for the stems of the plant materials. In this case, the curve at the tip of the handle points to exactly where the hole should be.

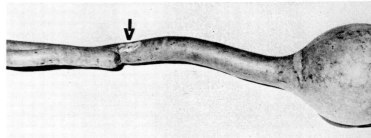

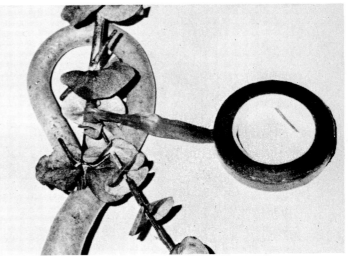

Place on stem of eucalyptus through the drilled hole into the gourd, the branch extending upward. Then tape the other branch onto the first stem slightly above the opening in the gourd.

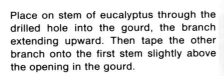

Wind the short stem of the dried flower with florist's tape and insert it into the hole in the gourd directly in front of the stems. Variation: Place a fresh flower into the water pick, then insert the pick into a large hole in the gourd.

Apply glue to the rim of the caster, then balance the bottom of the arranged gourd on the caster base. (See completed arrangement above.)

The radiating dried arrangement with stems of eucalyptus, red dried flowers, and statice is made in a Penguin gourd. The calabash container is painted with a red design at one end to match the color of the flowers.

To make a similar arrangement, cut an oval hole into the body of the Penguin gourd with a knife. Glue the gourd to a pedestal made from another gourd, wood, or a base made from another material.

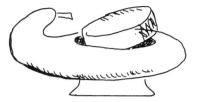

Slice the tall oval section of Styrofoam with a knife. Place the Styrofoam into the hole level with the opening in the gourd wall.

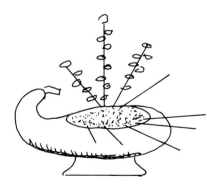

Establish radiating lines in the back of the gourd with long-stemmed plant material. Continue to push the shorter stems in the Styrofoam, bringing them around to the front.

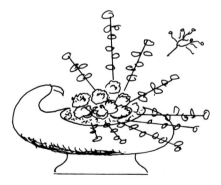

Place a triangular gathering of flowers at the base of the arrangement, from the largest flowers on the bottom to the smallest flower on top. Try not to place any two plants at the same height. To finish, add filler materials, baby's breath or statice where needed.

Crafted Flowers from Natural Materials. Lovely crafted flowers for sculptural arrangements can be made from cones, teasels, other pods, seeds, nuts, okra, and artichokes, cornhusks, ornamental corn, and Manila rope. Their parts can be glued together with fast-setting glues. Small cones and teasels (whole or halves) make good bases and centers for holding "petals." The coloring of crafted flowers made from natural materials usually blends well with gourds, though they may be accented with bright contrasting paints as well.

A crafted cornhusk Fuji Mum is the bright accent framed by the curved handle of the Dipper gourd. The winding Dipper gourd is suspended from the ceiling by a transparent strand of plastic fishing tackle. Dipper gourds can be grown into curved shapes on the ground. (See chapter 3.)

To make the cone-centered cornhusk Fuji Mum, you will need the following materials: *a.* eating corn with husks, *b.* a small cone (a hemlock cone or *Casuarina stricta,* a tropical prickly cone), *c.* steam iron, *d.* thick heavy stem wire and fine wire, *e.* florist's tape, *f.* hatpin, *g.* artificial leaf.

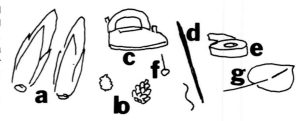

1

1. Preparing husks: Dry the innermost husks from eating corn separately between a couple layers of newspapers until they become white. Keep the husks in a dry place and allow the air to circulate around them so that they will not mildew.

2

2. When dry, iron each husk with a steam iron. If Accent spray paint is to be applied, add the color before ironing.

3

3. After you have protected the table's surface with a cutting board, you are ready to make the Fugi Mum. Have the ironed husks, hatpin, and scissors handy.

4

a.

hatpin

cut off tip

strip

husk

—strips

hold

b.

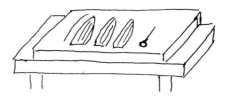

½ {

wire strips together

½ {

—12 strips of husk

c.

4. *a.* First cut off the pointed tip of each husk. Holding the broad stem end of the husk, cut very thin strips with a hatpin. *b.* You will need 108 strips. *c.* After dividing the strips into nine bunches, twelve strips each, take one bunch and wire them together in the middle with thin florist's stem wire.

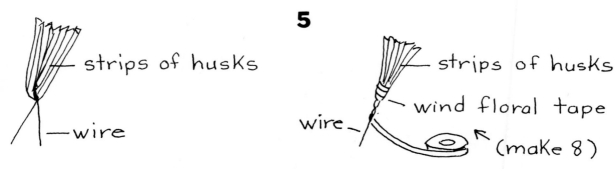

5

— strips of husks

—wire

strips of husks

— wind floral tape

wire ‾

↖ (make 8)

5. Fold the bottom half of the strip up, permitting the wires to extend down from the base of the bunch. While holding the folded strips together with one hand, wind floral tape over the folded base with the other. Diagonally tape from the base onto the wires about 1 inch. Then tape eight more bunches in the same manner.

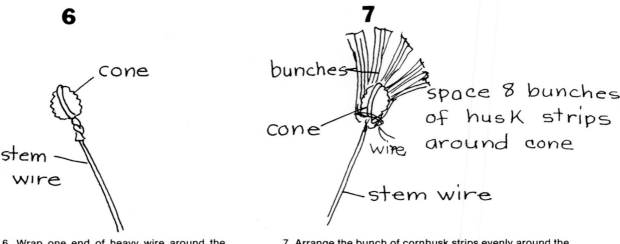

6

cone

stem
wire

7

bunches

cone

wire

space 8 bunches
of husk strips
around cone

stem wire

6. Wrap one end of heavy wire around the outside of the cone. Twist one end of the wire tightly onto the main stem wire directly beneath the cone using long-nosed pliers or wire cutters.

7. Arrange the bunch of cornhusk strips evenly around the base of the cone. Using thin wire, tie the bunches to the heavy stem wire at the base of the cone.

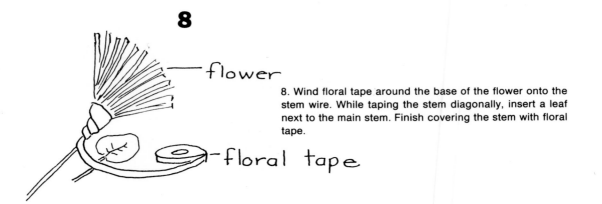

8

— flower

8. Wind floral tape around the base of the flower onto the stem wire. While taping the stem diagonally, insert a leaf next to the main stem. Finish covering the stem with floral tape.

— floral tape

Handcrafted flowers made from silky fibers of Manila rope and sliced Osage orange look well in gourd vases. Almost any type of center can be used for this flower, from sliced pinecones to Christmas ornaments and ribbon.

To make a Manila-hemp flower with an Osage orange center, you will need the following materials: *a.* Osage oranges (monkey balls), *b.* two 6-inch lengths of ⅜–½-inch Manila rope, *c.* 24-gauge florist's wire, *d.* wire cutters, *e.* heavy stem wire, *f.* white glue, *g.* long nail or ice pick, *h.* utility knife, *i.* sponge, *j.* comb, *k.* corn kernels (optional), *l.* fluorescent orange paint (optional), *m.* aluminum foil, *n.* baking sheet.

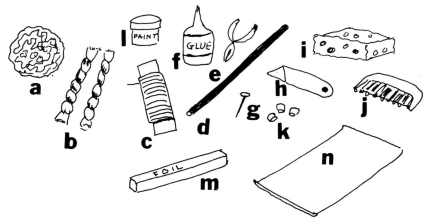

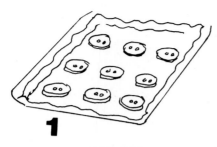

1

1. Cut the Osage oranges into approximate ¼-inch slices to make centers for the hemp flowers. Poke two holes in the center of each slice for the stem wire to go through later. Bake the slices on a cookie sheet lined with aluminum foil at 250 degrees until they are brown. Optional: When cool, glue some yellow corn kernels to the center of each slice. Then dab a little fluorescent orange paint over the kernels and around the edge of each slice.

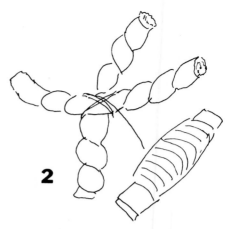

2

2. After cutting two 6-inch lengths of rope with a utility knife, cross the ropes in the center. Wind florist's wire, crisscrossing the center diagonally until the ropes hold together. When finished, tightly wind the spool wire to the free end of wire, but do not snip the wires from the spool yet.

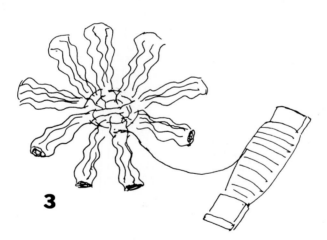

3

3. Unwind each rope into three strands. Then interspace each strand equally by winding wire around each rope at the center core of the flower. When finished, cut the wire and tie the end into the stitching.

4. Unravel the rope into separate strands and moisten the fibers with a wet sponge. After the water penetrates the fibers, comb the Manila fibers until they are straight.

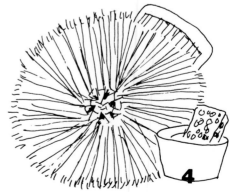

4

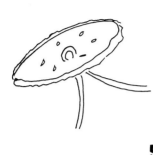

5

6

5. Next, bend a 14-inch strand of 24-gauge wire in the middle. Insert the ends of the curved wire through the holes in the Osage orange slice.

6. Make two holes in the center of the rope flowers with an ice pick or nail. Then insert the wires at the base of the Osage orange slice through the holes. Twist the wires together beneath the Manila flower.

2"

7

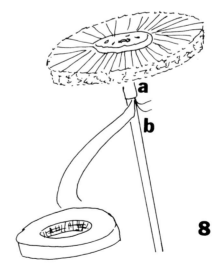

a

b

8

7. Cover the end of a heavy stem wire with 2 inches of floral tape.

8. Place the taped end of the stem under the center of the Manila flower next to the ends of the thin wires. Tape the two wires to the stem. *a.* Wind the tape horizontally beneath the flower a few times to hold it in place. *b.* Then continue taping diagonally down the rest of the stem.

The mosaic lamp base is methodically put together using sections from different gourds that vary in color and texture. Larue Stith

All-gourd lamp and shade. The body of the lamp is constructed by gluing the ball of the winding Dipper into a Tobacco Box gourd. The shade over the lamp fixtures is made from a large Kettle gourd. Geometric decoration on the shade and body of the lamp is burned with an electric wood burner. Larue Stith

Gourd lamp bases. *a.* plaster-weighted gourd without threaded pipe and base, *b.* gourd with threaded pipe inserted, *c.* narrow, long-necked gourd fitted with cork adapter, *d.* gourd globe suspended from a wooden swivel arm, *e.* globe gourd lamp suspended from vertical chain.

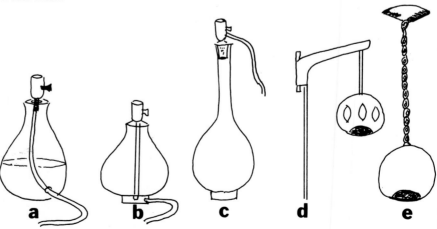

More Gourd Crafts and Accessories

Gourd Lamps

Mastering the techniques of gourd lamp making is relatively easy since a complete line of lamp parts is available at many hardware, all-purpose stores, and lamp shops. A single company manufactures a variety of separate components that fit well together when the lamp is constructed. For convenience, you can buy a kit that contains the necessary hardware and electrical wiring. Parts in the kit are constructed so that they can be placed easily on and through the gourd. Directions for electrical wiring, usually printed on the label, should be carefully followed so that the lamp can be used safely.

A necessary consideration with respect to lamp construction is weighting the gourd so that it will not topple easily. One option is to pour plaster of Paris or Sculptamold with gravel into the gourd. Another is to buy or make a heavy lamp base from hardwood, cast metal, or marble. Some manufactured lamp bases are hollow so that separate heavy lamp weights can be fitted inside.

A base purchased at a hardware store has a hole in the middle for the vertical pipe holding the cord. (See the drawing that shows the construction of the gourd lamp.) The opening in the base turns at a right angle so that the cord comes out one side. Here is one way to attach the lamp base to the bottom of the gourd. Insert the tip of the wire through the lamp base and inside the predrilled hole in the base of the gourd. Then pull the wire through the opening at the top of the gourd. Next thread the wire through a lamp pipe, which should have a nut screwed above the base of the pipe. After placing the lamp pipe through the inside into the hole at the base of the gourd, secure the tip of the pipe into the opening of the base. Tighten the nut inside the gourd to hold the lamp base secure.

Hanging globe lamp. Light passes through the colored glass globs, which are cemented into the precut openings of the Basketball gourd. Mrs. John L. Troutman

The globe lamp is decorated with painted flowers and drilled holes that allow the light to pass through. Mrs. John L. Troutman

A quick, easy way to make a gourd lamp is by fitting a reducible cork adapter or electrified candlestick with a rubber stopper into a gourd having a slightly smaller opening than the cork or stopper. Lamp parts with cork adapters are available in different sizes and can be fitted into smaller holes by cutting or peeling the cork. The cord that extends from the base of the socket can be hidden by placing it over the back of the lamp. The choice of an adapter with or without a harp depends on the type of shade to be used.

Shades that clip directly on the bulb are suitable over small gourds or on gourds with long and narrow necks. Shades and harps are proper for full-size gourds requiring a large shade. The lampshade used with a harp has a hole in the middle of the top wires that fits over the narrow threaded tip of the harp. The harp will raise the lampshade a couple of inches higher than a shade that is clipped on a bulb.

Choosing the right lamp parts depends on the size and shape of a particular gourd. The resulting overall proportions of the lamp and shade should have aesthetic appeal. Sometimes the shade should be raised high above the gourd for the best appearance. Since the threaded pipe will extend well above the top of the gourd, the pipe can be covered with brass tubing.

The most common parts that make up a quality gourd lamp from top to bottom are the finial, harp, socket, neck vase cap, threaded pipe, washer, nut, cord, and shade (base—optional). Not all these parts are needed in some lamps made from gourds.

172

Cork adapters are available with or
without harps.

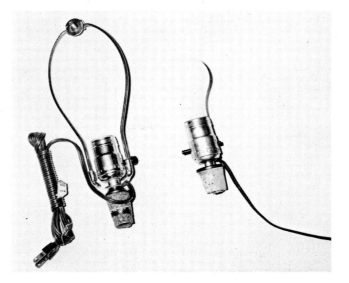

Lampshades. The first shade fits over a bulb and the
second over a harp.

Lamp parts: *a.* finial, *b.* harp, *c.* socket,
d. neck, *e.* vase cap, *f.* electrical wire,
g. threaded pipe.

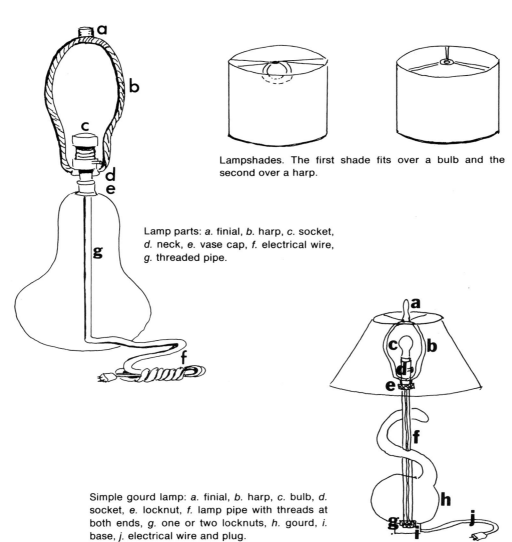

Simple gourd lamp: *a.* finial, *b.* harp, *c.* bulb, *d.*
socket, *e.* locknut, *f.* lamp pipe with threads at
both ends, *g.* one or two locknuts, *h.* gourd, *i.*
base, *j.* electrical wire and plug.

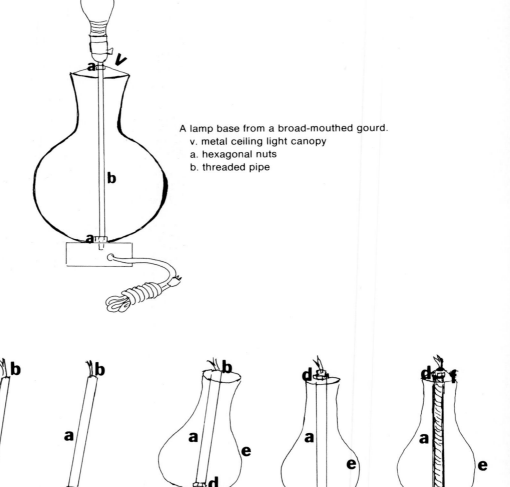

A lamp base from a broad-mouthed gourd.
  v. metal ceiling light canopy
  a. hexagonal nuts
  b. threaded pipe

a. threaded pipe, b. wire, c. base, d. nut, e. gourd, f. vase cap. 1. One way to make a lamp with a broad-mouthed gourd is to first thread the base and pipe with electrical wire. 2. Next, wind the nut down the threaded pipe to a position about 1½ inches from the bottom end. 3. After balancing the gourd on the lamp base, find a location on the bottom of the gourd for a hole through which the electric wire will run, then drill a hole large enough for the electrical wire. 4. Insert the threaded pipe through the inside of the gourd, down through the precut hole in the bottom of the gourd. Then push the tip of the threaded pipe through the hole in the lamp base. Be sure that the nut fits snugly on the top of the gourd's base. 5. After screwing another nut over the top of the pipe, fit the canopy over the top of the threaded pipe onto the opening of the gourd. If the canopy does not fit, shape it with a hammer. 6. Fit the socket over the pipe on the canopy and wire the socket according to the directions printed on the kit.

The abstract design on the lamp base has three contrasting colors: the white surface carved with a Dremel Moto tool (or hand-carving tool), broad black lines burned with a propane torch, and the natural coloring of the gourd wall. The white lampshade is trimmed at the top and bottom with gold and black braid. The lamp base is weighted inside with plaster. There is no long threaded pipe in this lamp, just a short one approximately 2 inches in length. Carolyn Mordecai

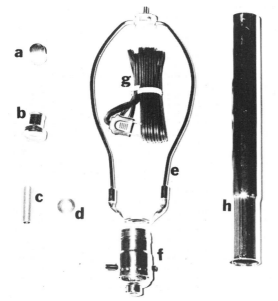

To make a similar lamp, you may need the following materials—a lamp kit that includes: *a.* finial, *b.* vase cap, *c.* threaded pipe, *d.* washer, *e.* harp, *f.* socket, *g.* electrical wire with plug, *h.* tubing to raise the socket and harp (optional).

Other materials and tools for making the carved and burned lamp. *Front row:* aluminum foil or plastic wrap, skewer, Dremel Moto tool with a ball carving tip or a hand-carving tool, knife, propane torch and lighter, freezer or masking tape; *second row:* linseed oil, plaster of Paris, bucket.

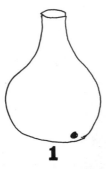

1

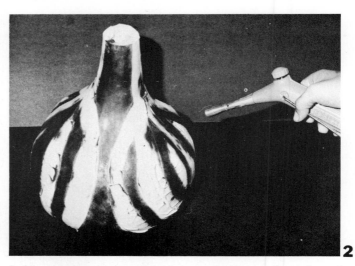

2

1. Cut off the top of the gourd to make a small opening for the lamp parts. Then drill or cut a hole in the bottom side of the gourd for the electrical wire. Wisk the interior of the gourd with a long skewer or wire to clean out the debris.

2. After drawing simple outlines for your design over the surface of the gourd, fill areas that are to remain the natural coloring of the gourd with two layers of freezer or masking tape. Leave exposed areas free to accept the burning from the flare of the torch. Use the torch according to the directions given in chapter 5. After the torch is lit, keep the knob turned to "lite." Use the lighted torch in a back and forth motion about 2 inches away from each opening. Avoid directing the flare of the torch over masked areas.

Apply linseed oil over the gourd wall.

3

3. When finished, remove the tape from the gourd's surface.

4. Carve the selected areas and lines, exposing the white layer beneath with the ball tip of a Dremel Moto tool or a hand-carving tool. It will be necessary to stop carving with the electric tool at intervals because the motor will get too hot.

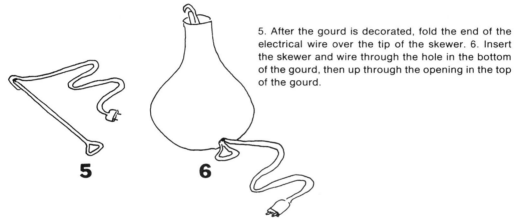

4

5

6

5. After the gourd is decorated, fold the end of the electrical wire over the tip of the skewer. 6. Insert the skewer and wire through the hole in the bottom of the gourd, then up through the opening in the top of the gourd.

7. To prepare for the pouring of the plaster, tape the extending end of the electrical wire to the top of the gourd.

7

8. Tape the hole in the bottom of the gourd where the electrical wire is threaded. Then protect the gourd with aluminum foil or Saran wrap.

9. After mixing enough water with the plaster to form a thick cream, immediately pour the mix into the opening at the top of the gourd. Clean the remaining plaster from the bucket with paper and throw it into a waste can. (Pouring plaster down the drain will cause the pipes to clog.) When finished, allow the plaster in the gourd to dry completely over a period of several days before constructing the rest of the lamp.

10

10. In order to find the screws in the socket for winding the tips of the electric cord, pull off the cup from the base of the socket. Then methodically follow the directions printed on the kit.

The socket fits on the threaded pipe, which is inserted into the opening at the top of the gourd. The vase cap is not used. Instead, the socket and pipe are held in place with a little more plaster. The plaster over the opening of the gourd may be painted to match the brown or black color of the lamp base.

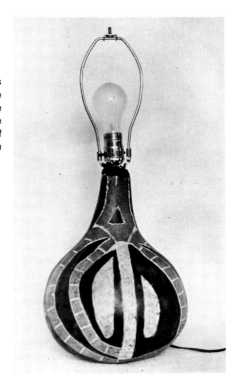

Gourd Jewelry

Leftovers from other gourd projects make interesting lightweight jewelry. Gourd shapes may be combined with jewelry findings to make bracelets, necklaces, and earrings. To add color or decoration to sections of gourd, brush on acrylic paints, oil paints, lacquers, or stain. Small prints may be applied with the decoupage medium, Mod Podge.

For the natural look, designs can be burned and/or engraved with a woodburning tool or electrical engraving tool shown in chapter 4. Beads may be wired or sewn on with plastic or other strong thread; or instead, they also may be glued inside a dent or opening in the gourd shell. Additional feathers, beads, shells, leather, bones, and stones give the jewelry a lively, natural look.

To create gourd jewelry, start by first drawing the shapes on white paper. Design simple shapes to avoid cracking of the gourd wall while the piece is being cut. Place the pattern over carbon paper and tape the sheets to the gourd shell. Then draw the patterns over the gourd wall.

If there is to be a preplanned opening in the middle of the gourd shape, drill or cut the opening before cutting out the piece. To cut out the shape, apply pressure with the pointed tip of a paring knife. Holding it perpendicular to the outline on the gourd, make short cuts in and out of the gourd shell, starting with points, angles, and narrow edges. Since most gourd walls are not flat, it is better to cut out the shapes for jewelry over the edge or corner of a table.

Finish the edges by smoothing them lightly with sandpaper or an emery board. If beading threads are to be used, make tiny holes through

The gourd necklace is made with cut and filed gourd sections, their edges burned with an electrical woodburning tool. After tiny holes in the gourd cutouts are made with a hatpin, the turquoise and white beads are strung to the gourd sections with plastic beading thread. A few curved strands of leather are glued over the surface of the gourd pendants.

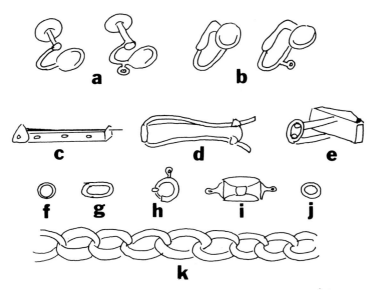

Jewelry findings. *a.* ear screws, *b.* ear clips, *c.* pin back, *d.* barrette, *e.* cuff link back, *f.* small wire circle, *g.* oval ring, *h.* spring ring, *i.* clasp, *j.* ring, *k.* chain.

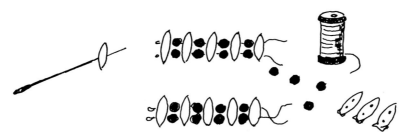

After two holes are pushed through each seed with a heavy sewing needle, a necklace or bracelet is made by inserting double strands of plastic beading thread through a seed, then two beads—alternately.

the gourd pieces where necessary with a heavyweight sewing needle. Avoid using an awl for making holes because the conical point tends to crack small sections of gourd.

The gourd shapes and the other decorative materials may be strung onto leather strands, braid, cord, or else on finer beading threads or plastic strands. Plastic beading threads are easily inserted through small holes in gourd shapes without using a needle. Jewelry findings may be applied to gourd shapes with a good crafts glue.

Pendant. The gourd pendant, strung onto a silky braid, is adorned with bark-stripped twigs backed with a coat of brown acrylic paint. Two sea urchin spines are suspended at the base of the pendant from wire rings.

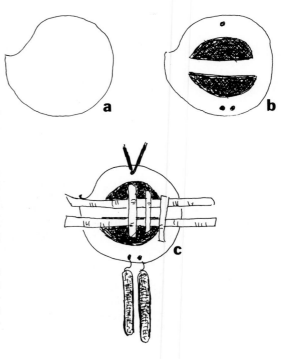

a. Cut a pendant shape from the gourd shell with the pointed tip of a paring knife. Always cut holding the knife perpendicular to the gourd's surface. If the gourd wall is curved, cut the piece over the edge of the table.

b. Push one hole through the top and two through the bottom of the gourd piece with a hatpin or other pointed tool. Paint a dark background design with acrylic or oil paint. Use a color, such as dark brown, that will complement the placement of the scraped twigs.

c. After scraping bark from the twigs with a paring knife, glue them into a pleasing design on the pendant. Suspend sea urchin spines or beads to the bottom of the pendant using wire circles.

182

The Bottle gourd necklace is made from small Bottle Lagenaria, rust-colored chicken feathers, shiny mahogany beads, and handles from Ornamental Spoon gourds. The materials are strung onto leather strands. The gourd shapes are still intact so that the necklace possesses a three-dimensional quality.

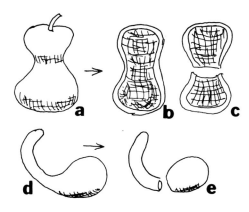

The whole a. Bottle gourd is cut in b. half. Just one of the halves of the gourd is cut into c. two quarters. d. The Spoon gourd's handle is e. cut off at the neck. The process is repeated with another Spoon gourd.

Bottle gourd necklace parts. a. leather strand, b. shiny mahogany beads, c. handle from Spoon gourd, d. ¼ small Bottle gourd, e. Bottle gourd, cut in half lengthwise, f. rust-colored chicken feathers, g. Turn the ½ Bottle gourd over to expose the inner gourd wall. Start making the necklace by knotting each long strand of leather in front of each hole in the upper chamber of the gourd. String the other materials on one side at a time: first a bead, then ¼ Bottle gourd shell with two predrilled holes in one end, a cleaned-out Spoon handle, and the last bead. Tie a knot after the last bead on each side. The necklace is worn by tying the leather strands together at the back of the neck.

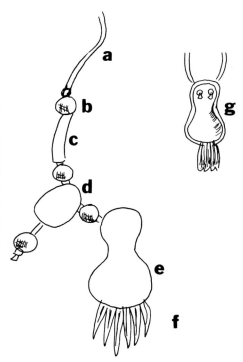

Musical Instruments from Gourds

For many centuries gourds have been used in the construction of musical instruments. Types vary from country to country. Generally, gourds are used as resonators to magnify the sound of musical instruments: they usually have an opening in the gourd wall for that purpose. Gourd string and percussion instruments are more prevalent than wind instruments. Though many instruments made with gourds are quite primitive, they are still being played in many parts of the world, particularly in Africa where most have originated. In the United States people enjoy making and playing simple lutes with gourd bodies and wooden necks. Not all gourd instruments are simplistic or primitive by nature. The exceptional and sophisticated sitar with its full range of expression is played by Hindustani musicians in the temples of India.

The most common of the gourd percussion instruments are the gourd rattles. Seeds inside the gourd are replaced by pebbles or seashells for a louder rattling sound. Some rattles have a loose netting of beads or shells covering the outside, and the rattling sound is obtained externally. Since there are so many kinds of instruments made from gourds, their names, the countries they come from, and descriptions are listed on the following chart:

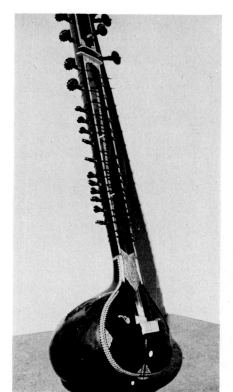

The sitar with its full range of expression is played by the Hindustani musicians in India. Courtesy, Museum of Marvin Johnson

PERCUSSION INSTRUMENTS

Name	Country	Description
Xylophone and Marimba	Mexico, Guatemala Ethiopia, Ghana, and southeast coast of Africa	Hard wooden keys increasing in size are placed over a series of graduated resonators. Each key has its own long narrow resonating gourd with a hole. The components are usually held together with cord. Sweet tones are produced by striking the wood keys with wood- or rubber-headed sticks.

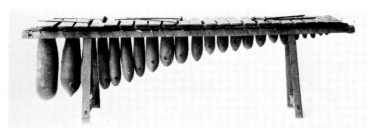

Guatamalan gourd marimba. Each hardwood key has its own resonating gourd. Similarly constructed gourd marimbas and xylophones are found in other Central American countries and in Africa. Courtesy, Smithsonian Institution

Thumb Piano	Sansa, Africa	Tongs, bamboo, wood, or metal keys— graduated in length— are constructed over one-half of a round gourd covered with a thin level board.

The Sansa-type thumb piano is African in origin. This thumb piano was made by an American craftsman, Peter Shapiro. Courtesy, Museum of Marvin Johnson

PERCUSSION INSTRUMENTS

Name	Country	Description
Drums Ipa Nui	Hawaii	The orchestra drum of Hawaii is an hourglass gourd or two gourds sewn together to create an hourglass chamber. An Ipa Nui gourd may be restricted in the center while it is growing. A hole 3 to 4 inches is cut at the top of the upper chamber. Its handle is often formed by tieing a strip of fabric around the middle. The Ipa Nui is played by striking it against the padded ground or by alternately hitting the gourd wall with the hand. The pitch is low and does not carry much sound. The Ipa Nui averages 12 to 22 inches in height and from 8 to 16 inches in diameter.

The hourglass Ipa Hula is an orchestra drum still being played in Hawaii.

Name	Country	Description
Kultrum or Ralecultrum	North American Indian	The kultrum is half of a calabash with animal skin stretched over the top. It was played by medicine men.
Rattles Maracas (originally a Brazilian name for gourds)	North and South America	The short-handled Dipper gourd is shaped by nature as a rattle. When the gourd seeds dry, the seeds will make a soft sound. Often pebbles were inserted through the stem end of the gourd to make the sound louder.

PERCUSSION INSTRUMENTS

Name	Country	Description
Dipper gourds with gourd or man-made handles	North and South America	A handle is placed in the stem end of a round gourd, or else the ball is sawed off the end of a dipper at the neck and the handle inserted. (See series of drawings on page 188.)
Chocalcho Asson	Central and South America	The chocalcho is shaped like the common gourd rattle that has a wooden handle, but this rattle has a loose network of beads over the gourd shell. When the rattle is shaken, the beads hit the gourd and produce a rattling sound.
Beaded net-covered rattle	African countries	A loose woven netting made with colorful beads, pieces of bamboo, or cowrie shells covers almost the entire gourd. The gourd rattle is made with a crooked-necked gourd, narrow at the stem end and swollen at the base. A small hole is cut near the top of the gourd resonator. When the gourd is shaken—the netting strikes against the gourd wall—it becomes one of the loudest rattles in all of Africa.

African gourd rattle from Cameroon. Beads, pieces of bamboo, or cowrie shells are strung onto a loose-fitted net over the gourd. These objects, striking against the external wall of the gourd, produce a loud rattling noise. Courtesy, Carnegie Institute, Museum Shops

PERCUSSION INSTRUMENTS

Name	Country	Description
Cabaca	Central and South America	The cabaca is made from a gourd that is restricted in the middle. The bottom half is covered with a loose network of beads. It is used as a rattle externally by either striking or shaking.

Painted gourd rattles from Equador.

Gourd rattles. *a*. Chocalcho or Asson of Central and South America, *b*. Jivaro Indian rattle from Equador, *c*. Polynesian rattle, *d*. North American Indian rattle, *e*. North American Indian rattle.

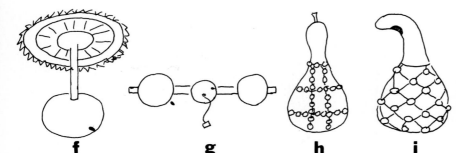

Gourd rattles. *f*. Hawaiian Uliuli with feathered handle, *g*. singing gourd rattle from Hawaii, *h*. beaded cabaca of South and Central America, *i*. large beaded rattle from Cameroon.

PERCUSSION INSTRUMENTS

Name	Country	Description
Polynesian	South Sea Islands	The round gourd top filled with seeds or pebbles has strips of ie drawn through four holes in the gourd. The strips of ie are pulled together, then tied with olona cord to form a handle.
Uliuli	Hawaii	The Uliuli, a rattle filled with seashells, has a round feathered fan at the tip of the handle. The rattle is held in one hand, then struck with the other.
Kani Nui "Singing Gourd" rattle	Hawaii	The "Singing Gourd" rattle is constructed by stringing three round gourds on a stick. Two larger gourds, containing pebbles, are attached permanently to each end of the stick. But the small center gourd, the hand-held section, moves freely on its axis. Coming from a hole in the small central gourd is a string. When it is pulled and released, the pebbles in the two outer gourds generate a sound. Successful operation will cause the string to automatically rewind itself.

PERCUSSION INSTRUMENTS

Name	Country	Description
Scrapers Guiro, gayo, or scraper	Cuba, Puerto Rico, Bahamas	A series of lines are filed into a Penguin-type gourd. Two openings are cut in the gourd, one at the top as a resonating hole and the other on the back to serve as a handle. The noise is made by scraping the serrations with a hardwood stick.
Gourd with notched stick	Southwest Indians of North America	A notched piece of wood is placed over a hole in the gourd resonator. It is in turn scraped with a stick to produce sound.

STRING INSTRUMENTS

Ughubu	African countries	The Ughubu is a single-stringed instrument made from a hunter's bow. The resonator is half of a round gourd secured near the base of the bent bow. The bow and resonator are held at the chest while the string is plucked with the hand or a sinew, a stick that is used as a bow. Sometimes the bow is fitted with a gourd rattle.

STRING INSTRUMENTS

Name	Country	Description
Kissar (harp)	Ethiopia, Uganda, Kenya	Two animal horns or sticks with a crossbar at the top are inserted into a round gourd resonator. From the crossbar are strings that descend vertically to the gourd. The strings are plucked with the fingers. Variation: Sometimes the front of the round gourd is sawed off and hide is stretched over the large opening. The strings descending from the crossbar are then stretched over the hide to the base of the gourd like a banjo's.
Gourd-resonated harp	African countries	An extended vertical of a right triangle, made from sticks, is set into the center of a round Cannonball gourd. The resonating hole is at the bottom of the gourd. The triangle on top of the gourd is fitted with seven fiber strings, graduating in length. The strings are plucked with the fingers.

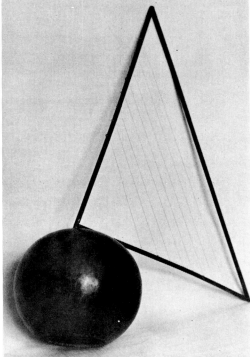

Gourd-resonated harp of Africa. The tones of the instrument are not rigidly controlled.

The gourd-resonated harp has an arm with pegs that allows some tone control. The halved gourd at the base is covered with skin that has a resonating hole. Courtesy, Museum of Marvin Johnson

STRING INSTRUMENTS

Name	Country	Description
Zither-lute or Vina	North American Indian	Two resonator gourds, 15 inches in diameter, are attached beneath both ends of a long wooden box or body. Running down the center of the long body are five strings with eight brass frets. There are two additional lateral strings. The zither lute is played in a kneeling position.

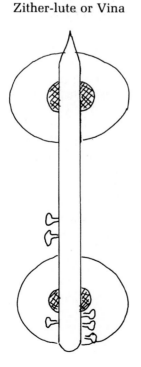

The body of the North American zither-lute. Strings run down the central long wooden box, which has a resonating gourd under both ends.

STRING INSTRUMENTS

Name	Country	Description
Travancor	South American Indian	The travancor is an elaborate form of zither-lute. Basically, it is a zither-lute with a pegbox at the top tipped with carved decoration. Beneath the pegbox is a painted gourd resonator. The bottom resonator is not a gourd, but a box made from hardwood. It has seven wire strings and three side strings drawn over twenty-four brass frets.
Veena (Vina)	India	The veena has a gourd body resembling that of a Western lute. Under the fretted neck near the pegs is a gourd resonator; often another hollow gourd resonator is fitted under the neck next to the main body. The sweet tones of the veena have subtle shadings and a full range of expression. They are obtained by plucking the seven-stringed instrument with the fingers or by using a plectrum over two fingers. Veenas vary in size and shape. Some older veenas were played with a bow.

Common parts of a string instrument. *a.* body, *b.* neck, *c.* bridge, *d.* resonating hole, *e.* frets, *f.* pegs, *g.* strings.

STRING INSTRUMENTS

Name	Country	Description
Sitar	India	Sitars have a gourd body with a long neck and are made similar to a veena. Since sitars vary in size according to the height of the musician, their tonal ranges and character change accordingly. Most sitars have six or seven main strings with eleven to thirteen sympathetic strings located in the neck under the main strings. The sympathetic strings resonate in tune when the main strings are plucked. The strings are played with a plectrum worn on the index finger as the sitarist sits in a special position on the floor or ground. The sitar has replaced the veena in northern India and is the popular stringed instrument of Hindustani musicians. Sitarists, usually accompanied by drums, play music for religious chants at Hindu and Sikh temples.

The strings of the sitar are played with a plectrum worn on the index finger.

The sitar from India may have two resonating gourds instead of one.

STRING INSTRUMENTS

Name	Country	Description
Surbahar	India	The surbahar is a deep-toned stringed instrument with a gourd body that is related to the sitar's. Its thick strings are several tones lower than the average sitar's.
Tamboura	India	The tamboura has a gourd body, but a neck with no frets. Its four to six strings are plucked without the use of a plectrum. The purpose of the tamboura is to sound tonic notes throughout a composition to provide awareness of the basic note of the raga.
Lute	African countries and United States	The lute has a resonating almond-shaped body made from a wood-covered halved gourd, or sometimes a whole gourd. The strings are stretched over the bridge on the body extending over the long neck to the pegs. The lute is played similar to a guitar. Lutes made from gourds are more primitive than the stringed instruments of India, such as the veena and sitar.

STRING INSTRUMENTS

Name	Country	Description
Guitar	United States	The body of a six-stringed (EBGDAE) guitar is made from two Canteen or Tobacco Box gourds. The upper gourd, 8 inches in diameter and 3¼ inches deep, is glued to the lower gourd, which is 7¼ inches wide and 8¼ inches thick. Parts of a guitar (perhaps from an old guitar) that are used for construction are the fingerboard, bridge, string holder, and strings. Cherry varnish is brushed on the body before the strings are placed on the **string** holder.
Violin	United States	The violin is constructed in the same manner as the guitar above. For the body, two Tobacco Box or Canteen gourds about 5½ inches in diameter and 3½ inches deep are used as well as standard violin parts: neck cover, fingerboard, string holder, and GDAE strings.

Violin created by Minnie Black. It is made from Mexican dumbell gourd. Courtesy, Minnie Black

WIND INSTRUMENTS

Name	Country	Description
Whistle	Hawaii	Whistles are made from gourds one to two inches in diameter. Each has two or three holes spaced at varying distances from the embrasure. Whistles are played by blowing air from the nose or mouth into the gourd. Most whistles produce two or three tones.
Flute	Ecuador	The flute of the Jibaro Indians in Ecuador is about 23 inches long. The long extension, 3 inches in diameter, contains a series of finger holes. It is tapered with a mouthpiece at the top and a gourd at the bottom.

Flute of the Jivaro Indians of Equador. Courtesy, Museum of Marvin Johnson

Name	Country	Description
Mouth Organ	Burma	A bundle of ten bamboo pipes of different lengths extends from a hole in the ball of a pipe-shaped gourd. Some of the pipes have finger holes. The mouthpiece is a roll of tin that is fitted at the stem end of the gourd.

The Gourd Drum

A drum can be made with almost any size gourd, cylindrical or round. The gourd is a resonator that receives vibrations from the drumhead when it is pounded. The larger the gourd, the deeper the sound will be.

Drumheads are usually made with rawhide. You may prepare a drumhead from animal skin or find ready-prepared drumheads at leather stores. Another resource of supply for heads are large music stores that repair broken drums. If an unusual size is needed, send to a drumhead or rawhide company and state the size and purpose.

After the drumhead is cut to size with a 1½- to 2-inch overlap over the edge of the open gourd, it may be glued, roped, tacked, braced, or buttoned to the gourd shell. The easiest method of creating a drum from a gourd is by tacking.

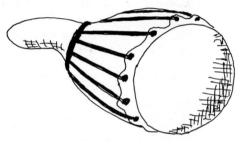

Gourd drum. The drumhead is laced to the body of the gourd.

The cylindrical Watermelon gourd drum receives vibrations from a commercially prepared rawhide drumhead. The rawhide is attached to the gourd resonator with upholstery tacks.

Saw or cut off the top of the gourd, then remove the seeds and pulp.

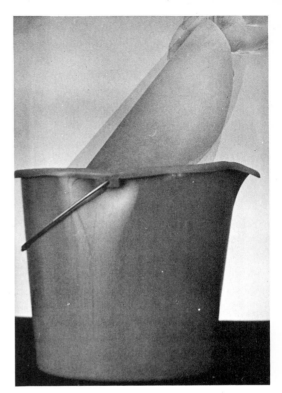

Soak the prepared hide in water for twelve hours. If necessary, cut the drumhead to size—1½ to 2 inches beyond the edge of the gourd.

Lay the water-soaked hide over the opening of the gourd. Allow the edge to fold over the side an equal distance from the rim. Push in the first tack through an opening in the rawhide into the side of the gourd. Without stretching the hide, tack the hide to the opposite side. Next, tack the rawhide to the edge between the two tacks already placed, then tack the opposite side. Continue tacking in this manner until the drumhead is completely attached. Remember that it is not necessary to stretch the hide, since prepared rawhide will shrink as it dries. After the head dries, be sure that the tacks are driven into the gourd before testing the drum.

Place the wet hide over several layers of folded newspapers. Make holes for the tacks at ¾–1-inch intervals around the edge of the hide by pounding an awl with a hammer.

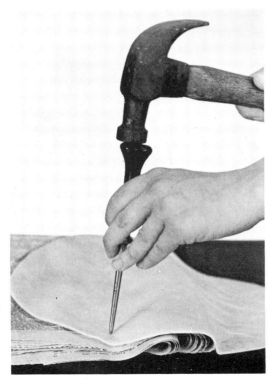

Birdhouses

Lagenarias make excellent homes for birds because the gourds endure all kinds of weather and require little construction. Since Hardshelled gourds grow into different sizes and shapes, it is easy to find one for the type of bird you wish to attract. Large gourds with long, deep cavities are suitable for large birds, such as woodpeckers and some small owls. A medium-sized gourd provides a good home for bluebirds and barn swallows. For smaller birds—chickadees, wrens, and titmice—a gourd 5 inches in diameter and 9 to 10 inches high is not too small.

In order to entice robins, phoebes, and song sparrows, one or more sides of the house should be open. Cut ample "windows" in the wall of the gourds for these birds.

After choosing the type of bird you wish to attract, select the gourd, and cut a round entrance hole, which should conform to the size of the particular bird. The following chart shows the minimum size gourd and the diameter of the entrance hole for each bird.

Gourd birdhouse with opening and perch. Courtesy, Gary Feuerstein

Name of Bird	Minimum Size Gourd	Diameter of Entrance Hole
	in Inches	in Inches
House or Bewick Wren	4	1
Caroline Wren	5	1⅛
Chickadee	4–6	1⅛–1¼
Tufted Titmouse	5	1½
Downy Woodpecker	5	1¼
White-breasted Nuthatch	5	1¼
Small Owl	5–6	1½
Bluebird	6–8	1¼
Owl	Very Large	5–6
Crested Flycatcher	6	2
Purple Martin	6	2½
Flicker	7	2½

Courtesy, Carroll Neidhart, American Gourd Society

In northern states hang the gourd birdhouse outside in the early spring before the birds arrive from the South. Place the house so that the opening is away from prevailing winds. When hanging several birdhouses, allow a reasonable amount of space between each one.

Though the majority of birds are not gregarious, martins and swallows enjoy living in closely knit groups. For them, just wire a cluster of gourds to bare branches of a tree or hang a number of houses from crossarms nailed to a pole. Be sure to keep their houses away from leafy vegetation and buildings.

Gourd birdhouses are easy to make and require few tools and additional materials: in addition to the gourd, you will need a stick or dowel for the perch, a sharp paring or pocket knife, and strong waterproof glue used for wood. Several basic birdhouses can be made in a short period of time. As you solve the housing problem, you will find our feathered friends grateful tenants.

A simple gourd birdhouse only needs an entrance hole, perch, small holes in the base for drainage, and openings in the top for the hanging device. The house can be made from almost any Lagenaria shape, as long as the gourd is large enough to house the birds.

Suggested materials for making the birdhouse include sandpaper, short dowel or stick, waterproof glue, compass or coin, pencil, knife with pointed tip, hanging device—wire or weatherproof cord, drill (optional), and plastic spray.

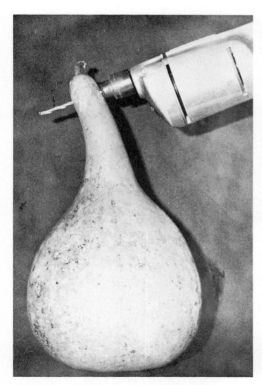

Drill holes straight through the top of the gourd for the hanging device.

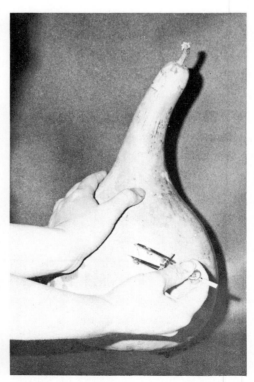

Draw the entrance hole high enough from the bottom of the gourd so that the bird can step down into the house.

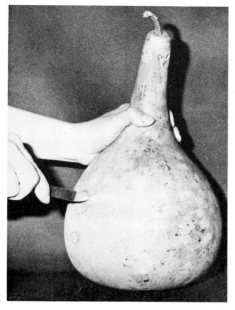

Cut open the entrance and perch holes with a knife.

Smooth the edge of the entrance hole with sandpaper or a sanding cylinder on a Dremel Moto tool.

After most of the seeds and pulp are removed from the gourd's interior, drill five to six small holes in the floor of the house to ensure drainage.

Glue the perch into the opening.

For a protective finish, apply one or two coats of shellac, varnish, or plastic spray.

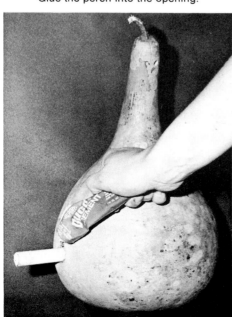

Bibliography
and a List of Supplementary References

Bailey, L. H. *The Garden of Gourds*. Boston, Massachusetts: Spaulding Moss, 1956.

Brandenburger, Nelda H. *Interpretive Flower Arrangement*. New York: Hearthside Press, Inc., 1969.

Dodge, Ernst S. *Gourd Growers of the South Seas*. Boston, Massachusetts: The Gourd Society of America, Inc., 1943.

Doty, L. Walter. *All About Vegetables*. San Francisco, California: Chevron Chemical Co., 1973.

Gourd Society of America, Inc., The. *Gourds, Their Culture & Craft*, 1966.

Ham'el and Sparkman. *Creativity with Gourds*. Saint Ignatius, Montana 59865: Ponderosa Publishers, 1971.

Howard, Dr. Joseph H. *Drums in the Americas*. New York: Oak Publications, 1967.

Jefferson, Louise E. *The Decorative Arts of Africa*. New York: Viking Press, 1973.

Keese, Allen. *The Sitar Book*. New York: Oak Publications, 1968.

Keynton, Tom. *Homemade Musical Instruments*. New York and London: Drake Publishers, 1975.

Lemos, Pedro J. *Guatemala Art Crafts*. Worcester, Massachusetts: The Davis Press, Inc., 1941.

Marcuse, Sibyl. *The Survey of Musical Instruments*. New York: Harper & Row, 1975.

Mason, Bernard S. *Crafts of the Woods*. Cranbury, New Jersey: A. S. Barnes & Company, 1973.

Menzie, Eleanor. *Hand Carved & Decorative Gourds of Peru*. Santa Monica, California: Karneke Publishers, 1976.

Newman, Thelma R. *Contemporary African Crafts.* New York: Crown Publishers, Inc., 1975.

Newman, Thelma R., Newman, Jay Hartley, and Newman, Lee Scott. *The Lamp & Lighting Book.* New York: Crown Publishers, Inc., 1976.

Octavio, Paz, and the World Crafts Council. *In Praise of Hands.* Greenwich, Connecticut: Contemporary Crafts of the World, New York Graphic Society, 1974.

Organ, John. *Gourds—Decorative and Edible for Garden, Craftwork, Table.* Newton, Massachusetts: Charles T. Branford Company, 1963.

Pearson, Harold E. *Pearson's Gourd Craft Manual.* El Monte, California, 1958.

Plummer, Beverly. *Earth Presents.* New York: Atheneum, 1974.

Rao, Harihar. *Introduction to Sitar.* New York: Peer International Corp., 1967.

Shankar, Ravi. *My Music, My Life.* New York: Simon & Schuster, 1968.

Speck, Frank. *The Gourd in Folk Literature.* Boston, Massachusetts: The Gourd Society of America, Inc., 1974.

———. *Gourds of the Southeastern Indians.* Boston, Massachusetts: The Gourd Society of America, 1941.

Stribling, Mary Lou. *Crafts from North American Indian Arts.* New York: Crown Publishers, Inc., 1975.

Toneyama, Kajin. *The Popular Arts of Mexico.* New York: John Weatherhill, Inc., 1972, 1974.

Trowel, Margaret. *African Design.* London: Faber & Faber, 1960.

Turnbull, Colin. *Musical Instruments of Africa.* New York: John Day Co., 1965.

Magazine Articles and Papers

"Gourds on Haiti." *The Gourd,* vol. 5, no. 3 (October 1975).

Hamlin, Mrs. Howard E. "Gourds, Their Culture & Use." American Gourd Society, Mount Gilead, Ohio.

MacIntyre, John W. "Gourds & Birds." First Unitarian Church, Bridgewater, Massachusetts.

Neidhart, Caroll. "Making Birdhouses from Gourds." American Gourd Society, Mount Gilead, Ohio.

Nichols Garden Nursery. "Gourds—Cultural and Growing Requirements." Albany, Oregon.

―――. "Profitable Gourd Crafting." Albany, Oregon.

"Old Maori Water Bottles, The." *Te Ao Hou,* The Maori Magazine, New Zealand (June 1962), pp. 38-40.

Rubin, Dr. Barbara. "Calabash Decoration in North East State Nigeria." *African Arts,* IV, 1 (Autumn 1970), pp. 21–24.

Schoon, Theo. "Growing Maori Gourds." *Te Ao Hou,* The Maori Magazine, New Zealand (June 1962), p. 59.

"So Your Gourds Rotted: Or Did They?" American Gourd Society, Mount Gilead, Ohio.

Sterling, H. P. "Speeding Up Sprouts." American Gourd Society, Mount Gilead, Ohio.

Stevens, John. "Lagenarias." *The Gourd,* vol. 5, no. 1 (February 1975).

Stevens, Mrs. O. C., and Miller, Mrs. Leslie. "Gourd Seed and Planting." American Gourd Society, Mount Gilead, Ohio.

Voelm, Mrs. C. H. "A Guitar from a Gourd." *The Gourd,* vol. 5, no. 2 (June 1975).

―――. "A Violin from a Gourd." *The Gourd,* vol. 5, no. 1 (February 1975).

Williams, Dr. Louis O. "The White Flowered Bottle Gourd." *The Gourd,* vol. 4, no. 2 (June 1974).

Sources of Supplies

Batik Waxes

Pure Beeswax
Ukrainian Gift Shop
2422 Central Avenue, N.E.
Minneapolis, Minnesota
55418

Batik Wax
Macmillan Arts & Crafts, Inc.
9520 Baltimore Avenue
College Park, Maryland
20740

The Batik Art Place
530 A Miller Avenue
Mill Valley, California 94941

Beads

Walco Products
1200 Zerega Avenue
Bronx, New York 10462

Bead Game (assorted beads)
505 North Fairfax Avenue
Los Angeles, California 90036
(catalog)

Brayer (hand roller)

Speedball
Hunt Manufacturing Co.
Statesville, North Carolina
28677

Clock Movements

National Artcraft Supply Co.
12213 Euclid Avenue
Cleveland, Ohio 44106

Decorated Gourds

Peruvian Gourds
Raquel's Collection
4 North Road
Great Neck, New York 11024

Sergio Carvajal
PRECOLUMBIAN JEWELS
5533½ Walnut Street
Pittsburgh, Pennsylvania
15232

Mexican Gourds
Mexican Folk Art
Annex, Inc.
23 West 56th Street
New York, N.Y. 10019

Decoupage

Harrower House of
Decoupage
37 Carpenter Street
Milford, New Jersey 08849
(Catalog $1)

Drills

Dremel Moto-Tool Kit
Dremel Manufacturing Co.
4915 21st Street
Racine, Wisconsin 53406

Craftsman Portable Drill
Sears, Roebuck & Company

Drumheads

Tandy Leather
Stores throughout U.S.

Floral-arranging Supplies

Floral Art
467 Main Street
Dennis, Massachusetts 02638

Gourd Seeds

Nichols Garden Nursery
(highly recommended—very
good seed)
1190 North Pacific Highway
Albany, Oregon 97321

Stokes Seeds, Inc.
Box 548, Main P.O.
Buffalo, New York 14240

W. Atlee Burpee Company
P.O. Box 6929
Philadelphia, Pennsylvania
19132

George W. Park Seed Co.,
Inc.
P.O. Box 31
Greenwood, South Carolina
29647

Hardware

Small Hinges and Handles
Brainerd Manufacturing Co.
East Rochester, New York
14445

Latches—1" Hooks and Eyes
National
Sterling, Illinois 61081

Swivel Locks
Tandy Leather
Stores throughout U.S.

India Ink

Higgins
Faber-Castell Corporation
Newark, New Jersey 07103

Jewelry Findings

National Artcraft
Supply Company
12213 Euclid Avenue
Cleveland, Ohio 44106

Knives, Blades, Handles, Gouges

X-acto, Inc.
48-51 Van Dam Street
Long Island City, New York
11101

Lamp Parts

National Artcraft Supply Co.
12213 Euclid Avenue
Cleveland, Ohio 44106

Leather Dyes

Tandy Leather
Cities throughout U.S.

Tandy Leather Dyes (water-
based dye that produces
pastel colors on gourds)

Fiebing's Leather Dyes
(absorbent solvent-based dye
that produces deep colors)

Macramé Cords and Beads

American Handicrafts
Cities throughout U.S.

The Weaver's Place
Dickey Mill, 4900
Wetheredsville Road
Baltimore, Maryland 20207

Mod Podge (quick decoupage formula)

Connoisseur Studio, Inc.
Box 7187
Louisville, Kentucky 40207

Music Box Movements and Turnable Bases

National Artcraft Supply
Company
12213 Euclid Avenue
Cleveland, Ohio 44106

Paints

Acrylic Paints
LIQUITEX
Permanent Pigments
27000 Highland Avenue
Cincinnati, Ohio 45212

Lacquer Enamels
Sherman Williams (order by
the gallon)

Wolf Paints
771 Ninth Avenue
New York, New York 10019

Oil Paints
Grumbacher, Inc.
460 West 34th Street
New York, New York 10001

*Oils, Acrylics, Gloss Plastic
Spray, Gloss Medium, Gel
Medium*
Cappy and Company
14 Wood Street
Pittsburgh, Pennsylvania
15222 (catalog)

Pen

(Artist's drawing pen—
available at good art or
drafting stores)

*Castell Technical Pen and
Points* or
*Rapidograph Technical Pen
and Points*
Cappy and Company
14 Wood Street
Pittsburgh, Pennsylvania
15222 (catalog)

Rub 'n Buff Metallic Paste

Rub 'n Buff Division
American Art Clay Co., Inc.
Indianapolis, Indiana 46268

Sculptamold, AMACO ®

American Art Clay Co., Inc.
4717 West Sixteenth Street
Indianapolis, Indiana 46222

Tent Pegs

Army-navy stores

Wax

Johnson's Paste Wax
S. C. Johnson and Son, Inc.
Racine, Wisconsin 53403

Weaving Fibers

The Weaver's Place
Dickey Mill
4900 Wetherdsville Road
Baltimore, Maryland 21207

The Hidden Village
225A Yali Avenue
Claremont, California
(Catalog $1)

Naturalcraft
2199 Bancroft Way
Berkeley, California 94704

Woodburning Tool

Electrical Wood Burner
No. 400647 (3 burning tips)
Leisure Dynamics, Inc.
Minneapolis, Minnesota
55435

Index